C++ PROGRAMMING

MIKE McGRATH

In easy steps is an imprint of Computer Step
Southfield Road . Southam
Warwickshire CV47 0FB . United Kingdom
www.ineasysteps.com

Notice of Liability
Every effort has been made to ensure that this book contains accurate and current information. However, Computer Step and the author shall not be liable for any loss or damage suffered by readers as a result of any information contained herein.

Trademarks
All trademarks are acknowledged as belonging to their respective companies.

Printed and bound in the United Kingdom

ISBN 1-84078-295-1

Contents

Introducing C++

Welcome to the exciting world of C++ programming. This initial chapter introduces the C++ language. A simple example demonstrates how to create a program, how to compile it into machine-readable byte code, then how to execute the finished program.

Covers

Chapter One

The C++ programming language

C++ is an extension of the C programming language which was first implemented on the UNIX operating system by Dennis Ritchie in 1972. C is a flexible programming language that remains popular today and is used on a large number of platforms for everything from microcontrollers to the most advanced scientific systems.

C++ was developed by Dr. Bjarne Stroustrup between 1983–1985 while working at AT&T Bell Labs in New Jersey. He added features to the original C language to produce what he called "C with classes". These classes define programming objects with specific features that transform the procedural nature of C into the object–oriented programming language of C++.

The C programming language was so named as it succeeded an earlier programming language named "B" that had been introduced around 1970. The name "C++" displays some programmers' humor because the programming ++ increment operator denotes that C++ is an extension of the C language.

C++, like C, is not platform-dependent so programs can be created on any operating system. Most illustrations in this book depict program output on the Windows operating system purely because it is the most widely used desktop platform. The examples can also be created on other platforms such as Linux or MacOS.

Why learn C++ programming?

The C++ language is favored by many professional programmers because it allows them to create fast, compact programs that are robust and portable.

Using a modern C++ Integrated Development Environment (IDE), such as Borland's C++ Builder or Microsoft's Visual C++, the programmer can quickly create complex applications. But to use these tools to greatest effect the programmer must first learn quite a bit about the C++ language itself.

This book is an introduction to programming with C++, giving examples of program code, and its output, to demonstrate the basics of this powerful language.

Should I learn C first?

Opinion is divided on the question of whether it is an advantage to be familiar with C programming before moving on to C++. It would seem logical to learn the original language first in order to understand the larger extended language more readily. However, C++ is not simply a larger version of C as the approach to object–oriented programming with C++ is markedly different to the procedural nature of C. It is, therefore, arguably better to learn C++ without previous knowledge of C to avoid confusion.

This book makes no assumption that the reader has any previous knowledge of any programming language so is suitable for the beginner to programming in C++, whether they know C or not.

If you do feel that you would benefit from learning to program in C before moving on to C++ try the examples in "C Programming in easy steps" before reading this book.

Standardization of C++

As the C++ programming language gained in popularity it was adopted by many programmers around the world as their programming language of choice. Some of these programmers began to add extensions to the language so it became necessary to agree upon a precise version of C++ that could be commonly used internationally by all programmers.

"ISO" is not an acronym but is derived from the Greek word "isos" meaning equal, as in "isometric".

A standard version of C++ was defined by a joint committee of the American National Standards Institute (ANSI) and the Industry Organization for Standardization (ISO). This version is sometimes known as ANSI C++ and is portable to any platform and any development environment.

The examples given in this book conform to ANSI C++. Example programs run in a console window, such as a Command Prompt window on Windows systems or a terminal window on Linux systems, to demonstrate the mechanics of the C++ language itself. An example in the final chapter illustrates how code generated automatically by a visual development tool on the Windows platform can, once you're familiar with the C++ language, be edited to create a graphical windowed application.

C++ compilers

C++ programs are initially created as plain text files, saved with the file extension of ".cpp". These can be written in any text editor, such as Windows' Notepad application or EMACS on Linux – no special software is needed.

In order to execute a C++ program it must first be "compiled" into byte code that can be understood by the computer. A C++ compiler reads the text version of the program and translates it into a second file – in machine-readable executable format.

Should the text program contain any syntax errors these will be reported by the compiler and the executable file will not be built.

If you are using the Windows platform and are lucky enough to have a C++ Integrated Development Environment (IDE) installed then you will already have a C++ compiler available as the compiler is an integral part of the visual IDE. The Microsoft Visual C++ IDE provides an editor window, where the program code can be written, and buttons to compile and execute the program. Visual IDEs can, however, seem unwieldy when starting out with C++ because they always create a large number of "project" files that are used by advanced programs.

At the time of writing Borland offer the C++ compiler that is used by their C++ Builder visual IDE for free download from http://www.borland.com/products/downloads. This is an executable file named bcc32.exe that runs from the command line.

The complete terms and conditions of the General Public License can be found at http://www.gnu.org/copyleft/gpl.html

The popular GNU C++ compiler is available free under the terms of the General Public License (GPL). It is included with virtually every distribution of the Linux operating system. The GNU C++ compiler is also available for Windows platforms and has been used to compile every example given in this book.

To discover if you already have the GNU C++ compiler on your system type c++ -v at a command prompt. If it's available the compiler will respond with version information. If you are using the Linux platform and the GNU C++ compiler is not available on your computer install it from the distribution CD-ROM, or ask your system administrator to install it for you. Windows users will need to install the GNU C++ compiler by following the instructions on the next page.

GNU is a recursive acronym for "GNU's Not Unix".

The GNU (pronounced "guh-NEW") Project was launched in 1984 to develop a complete free Unix-like operating system. A part of the GNU system is the Minimalist GNU for Windows (MinGW). MinGW includes the GNU C++ Compiler that can be used on Windows systems to create executable C++ programs.

MinGW download information can be found at
http://www.mingw.org/download.shtml
and the package can be downloaded from
http://sourceforge.net/project/showfiles.php?group_id=2435

The MinGW distribution is an executable file named something like MinGW-3.1.0-1.exe.

MINGW_3_1_0 _1.EXE

After downloading the file, run the installation and accept the suggested default location of C:\MinGW.

On older versions of Windows add the C:\MinGW\ bin address at the end of the Set Path statement in the C:\autoexec.bat file.

The final step is to add the C:\MinGW\bin subdirectory of the MinGW installation to your system Path. In Windows XP open the Environment Variables dialog by clicking the System icon in the Control Panel, then select the Advanced tab and push the Environment Variables button. Find the Path variable then edit the end of its statement line to include the address C:\MinGW\bin.

To verify that installation completed properly, at a command prompt type c++ --help to see the compiler command options or type c++ -v to see the GNU C++ compiler respond with version information, something like the illustration below. If you do not see this, reboot your computer, check the environment variables then retry the commands.

A first C++ program

In C++ programs the code statements to be executed are contained inside "functions". Code that defines a function is called a function "declaration" and always has this syntax:

```
data-type function-name() { statements-to-be-executed }
```

Avoid choosing names that begin with an underscore as some C++ libraries use that naming convention.

After a function has been called upon to execute the statements it contains, it returns a value to the caller. This value can only be of the data-type specified in the function declaration.

A program can contain one or many functions but must always have a function called "main". The main function is the starting point of all C++ programs and the compiler will not compile the code unless it finds a function called "main" within the program.

Other functions in a program can be given any name you like using letters, digits and the underscore character, but the name may not begin with a digit. Also the C++ keywords, listed in the Handy Reference on the inner front cover of this book, must be avoided.

The plain brackets that follow the function-name can, optionally, contain values to be used by that function. These take the form of a comma-separated list and are known as function "arguments".

After typing the final closing brace always hit the Enter key to add a newline at the end of the file – your compiler may insist that a source file should end with a newline character.

The curly brackets (braces) contain the statements to be executed whenever the function is called. Each statement must be terminated by a semi-colon, in the same way that English language sentences must be terminated by a full stop.

Traditionally, the first program to attempt when learning any programming language is that which simply generates the message "Hello World". In C++, the program code looks like this:

hello.cpp

```cpp
#include <iostream>
using namespace std;

int main()
{
    cout << "Hello World\n";
    return 0;
}
```

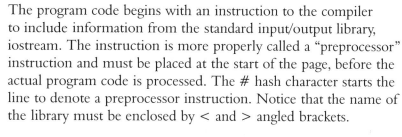

Notice how the program code is formatted using spacing and indentation (collectively known as whitespace) to improve its readability. All whitespace is completely ignored by the C++ compiler.

The program code begins with an instruction to the compiler to include information from the standard input/output library, iostream. The instruction is more properly called a "preprocessor" instruction and must be placed at the start of the page, before the actual program code is processed. The # hash character starts the line to denote a preprocessor instruction. Notice that the name of the library must be enclosed by < and > angled brackets.

The second line of the program makes all the functions within the iostream library available for use by their standard names, which are in the namespace std. One of these is a function named cout that is used to write the output from a program.

In the function declaration the data-type is specified as int, meaning integer. This means that after executing its statements this function must return an integer value to the operating system.

As this program contains just one function it must be named as the obligatory main function that is required in all C++ programs. The plain brackets after the main function-name are empty as no optional arguments have been specified.

Each statement must be terminated with a semi-colon.

The braces contain the statements to be executed by the program. The first statement calls upon the cout function that is defined in the standard input/output iostream library. The << operator specifies a string of text to be written to standard output by cout. Notice that in C++ programming, strings must <u>always</u> be enclosed in double quotes. This string contains the text "Hello World" and the newline escape sequence \n. This is one of the escape sequences listed in the Handy Reference on the inner front cover of this book. It will move the print head to the left margin of the next line following output of the "Hello World" text.

The final statement in the main function uses the C++ return keyword to return a value of zero to the operating system. Traditionally returning a zero value after the execution of a program indicates to the operating system that the program executed correctly.

The program in text format is saved with the ".cpp" file extension as hello.cpp and is ready to be compiled to create an executable version in machine-readable byte code format.

Compiling and running programs

The C++ source code files for the examples in this book are stored in a directory created expressly for that purpose. The directory is named "MyPrograms" – its absolute address on Windows is C:\MyPrograms, on Linux it's /home/MyPrograms.

The hello.cpp program source code file, created on page 12, is saved in this directory awaiting compilation to produce a version in executable byte code format.

At a command prompt type c++ --help to see a list of all the possible compiler options.

From a command prompt navigate to the MyPrograms directory, then type c++ hello.cpp to attempt to compile the C program. When the attempt succeeds the compiler creates an executable file alongside the original source code file. By default this file will be called a.exe on Windows systems (a.out on Linux systems).

Compiling a different C++ source code file in the MyPrograms directory would now overwrite the first executable file without warning. This is obviously unsatisfactory so a custom name for the executable file must be specified when compiling hello.cpp.

To make the compiler generate an executable file with a specific name use its -o option, followed by your preferred file name.

The command c++ is an alias for the GNU C++ compiler – the command gcc also calls the compiler.

On either Windows or Linux platforms now type the command c++ hello.cpp -o hello.exe at a prompt in the MyPrograms directory. This will compile the hello.cpp source code file and generate an executable file named hello.exe.

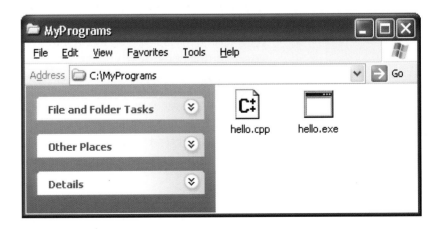

All the code examples in this book have been compiled and tested with both the GNU C++ compiler (version 3.2) and Microsoft Visual C++ 6.0 – they are not assured to work on other versions, compilers or platforms.

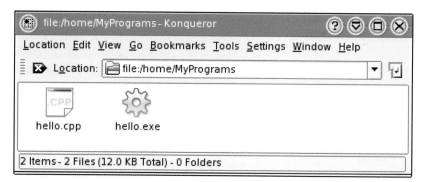

To run the generated executable program file in Windows simply type the file name hello.exe at the command prompt in the MyPrograms directory.

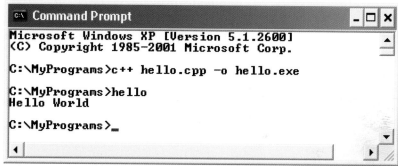

Windows users can even omit a file extension to run programs. In this case, just typing hello is sufficient.

Because Linux does not, by default, look in the current directory for executable files, unless it is specifically directed to do so, it is necessary to prefix the file name with ./ to execute the program.

Adding comments

It is good programming practice to add comments to your C++ source code. This makes the code more easily understood when read by other people, or by yourself when revisiting a piece of code after a period of absence.

Any remarks on a single line following a // double slash are ignored by the C++ compiler.

The /* ... */ comment syntax is carried over from the C language. It is recommended that C++ programs use the newer // comment syntax.

Also any remarks that appear between /* and */ are ignored by the compiler, even when spread across multiple lines.

Most commercial C++ programs begin with a comment block describing the purpose of the program together with other information such as the author's name, date the program was written, copyright permissions and so on.

Comments may also describe the purpose of individual functions and statements. The previous program hello.cpp, listed on page 12, could be enhanced with useful comments like those below:

hello.cpp
(commented)

```
/*
    This is a first program to introduce C++ programming.
    Its purpose is to generate the traditional message
    of "Hello World", then move on to a new line.
*/

/* First make the standard input/output functions
    in the iostream library available to this program.
*/
#include <iostream>
using namespace std;

// declare the obligatory main() function
int main()
{

    // call the cout function to output a string
    cout << "Hello World\n";

    // return zero to confirm that the program ran ok
    return 0;
}
```

This is ideally how C++ source code should be commented – the examples in this book are largely uncommented, however, because of space limitations.

Storing data

This chapter introduces the various ways to store data for manipulation within a C++ program. Examples demonstrate how to store both variable and constant data and illustrate how to store multiple items of data in arrays and vectors.

Covers

Chapter Two

Creating variables

A variable is like a container in a C++ program in which a data value can be stored inside the computer's memory. The stored value can be referenced using the variable's name. The programmer can choose any name for a variable providing it follows the naming conventions listed in the table below:

Variable names are case-sensitive in C++ – so variables named "Var", "VAR" and "var" would be treated as three separate variables by the program. Traditionally C++ variables use lowercase.

Naming rule	Example	Accept
Cannot start with a number	2bad	No
Can contain a number elsewhere	good4	Yes
Cannot contain arithmetical operators	a+b*c	No
Cannot contain punctuation characters	%$#£@!	No
Can contain the underscore character	_is_good	Yes
Cannot contain any spaces	no spaces	No
Can be of mixed case	UPdown	Yes
Cannot contain any C++ keywords	class	No

C++ keywords are listed on the inner front cover of this book.

It is good practice to choose meaningful names for variables to make the program more easily understood.

To create a variable in a program requires it to be "declared". A variable declaration has this syntax:

```
data-type variable-name ;
```

First the declaration specifies which type of data the variable is permitted to contain. This will be one of the data types described on the opposite page. The type is followed by a space then the chosen variable name, adhering to the naming rules. Finally the declaration is terminated by a semi-colon. This is used much like a full stop in the English language to mark the end of a sentence. Multiple variables of the same data type can be created in a single declaration by separating the variable names with a comma:

```
data-type variable1, variable2, variable3 ;
```

There are five basic data types in the C++ language. These are defined using the C++ keywords which are listed in the following table, together with a description of each data type:

Additionally C++ provides a special string data type that can contain strings of characters. This is demonstrated in Chapter 5 – "Working with strings".

Data type	Description	Example
char	a single byte, capable of holding one character	A
int	an integer whole number	100
float	a floating-point number, correct up to six decimal places	0.123456
double	a floating-point number correct up to ten decimal places	0.0123456789
bool	a boolean value of true or false, or numerically any non-zero value represents true and zero represents false	false (0) true (-1)

The five data types allocate different amounts of machine memory for storing data. A char is the smallest and the largest is a double. A double is twice the size of a float so should be used only when a precise lengthy floating point number is necessary.

Variable declarations are made before any executable code. When a value is assigned to a variable that variable is said to have been "initialized". Optionally a variable may be initialized when it is declared. The example code fragment below creates a variety of variables and initializes them with appropriate values:

```
int num1, num2;            //declare 2 int variables
char letter;               //declare a char variable
double longnum;            //declare a double variable
float decimal = 7.5;       //declare and initialize float
bool flag = true;          //declare and initialize bool

num1 = 100;                //initialize the int variables
num2 = 200;

letter = 'A';              //initialize char variable
longnum = 1.0987654321;    //initialize double variable

flag = false;              //assign new boolean value
```

Values of the char data type must always be enclosed by single quotes – double quotes are incorrect.

Displaying variable values

The value of variables can be displayed using the cout function that was used in Chapter 1 to display the "Hello World" message. The value stored in each variable is substituted for the variable name in the output.

The example program below creates and initializes variables of each of the five basic C++ data types listed on the previous page then displays each stored value. Newline characters are added at the end of each line of this output by the endl statement. This can be used as an alternative to the \n escape sequence.

firstvars.cpp

```cpp
#include <iostream>
using namespace std;

int main()
{
  int num = 100;
  char letter = 'M';
  float decimal = 7.5;
  double pi = 3.14159;
  bool flag = false;

  cout << "num:\t" << num << endl;
  cout << "letter\t" << letter << endl;
  cout << "decimal:" << decimal << endl;
  cout << "precise:" << pi << endl;
  cout << "flag\t" << flag << endl;
  return 0;
}
```

The \t tab escape sequence is used in this example to align the generated output.

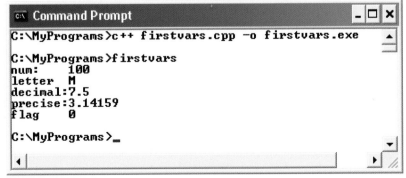

Notice that the output for the bool variable is expressed numerically as 0. A true value would typically be output as 1.

Inputting variable values

The cout function that is used to generate output has a corresponding function named cin that is used to get user input. The input data can be assigned to appropriate variables then manipulated by the program.

This simple example gets two integer values from the user then outputs the total when they have been added together:

setvars.cpp

```cpp
#include <iostream>
using namespace std;

int main()
{
    int num1, num2, total;

    cout << "Hi! Enter a number: ";
    cin >> num1;
    cout << "Now enter another number: ";
    cin >> num2;
    total = num1 + num2;
    cout << "Your numbers total " << total << endl;

    return 0;
}
```

The cin function has two >> "greater than" characters to signify input – whereas cout has two << "less than" characters to signify output.

```
C:\MyPrograms>c++ setvars.cpp -o setvars.exe

C:\MyPrograms>setvars
Hi! Enter a number: 28
Now enter another number: 12
Your numbers total 40

C:\MyPrograms>_
```

This example can be made more efficient by declaring just two int variables and reassigning the sum of the two input integers to one of these variables. For instance, declaring just num1 and num2 the sum is reassigned to num1 with the code num1 = num1 + num2; – the final cout statement can then output num1 to show the total.

Data type qualifiers

The range of possible int values is determined by your system. If the int variable is created by default as a "long" type it typically will permit a range of values from +2,147,483,647 to -2,147,483,648. On the other hand, if the int variable is created by default as a "short" type then typically the range will be +32,767 to -32,768.

The range can be explicitly specified when declaring the variable by prefixing the int keyword with the short or long qualifier keywords, followed by a space. The short int is useful to save on memory space when you are sure its range will not be exceeded.

When an int variable is declared it can by default contain either positive or negative integer values. These are known as "signed" values. If the variable will always contain only positive integers a non-negative "unsigned" int can be declared with the unsigned keyword. An unsigned short int variable will typically have a possible range from 0 to 65,535. An unsigned long int variable will typically have a possible range from 0 to 4,294,967,295.

See page 43 for more examples using the sizeof operator.

The sizeof operator is used in this example to examine the amount of memory space allocated to int data types:

sizeof.cpp

```
#include <iostream>
using namespace std;

int main()
{
  cout << "short int: "<<sizeof(short int)<<" bytes\n";
  cout << "long int: " << sizeof(long int)<<" bytes\n";
  cout << "default int: " <<   sizeof(int)<<" bytes\n";
  return 0;
}
```

Here the int variable is created as a "long" type – your system may be different.

```
C:\MyPrograms>c++ sizeof.cpp -o sizeof.exe

C:\MyPrograms>sizeof
short int: 2 bytes
long int: 4 bytes
default int: 4 bytes
```

Arrays

An array is a variable that can store multiple items of data, unlike a regular variable which can only store a single item of data. The pieces of data are stored sequentially in array "elements" that are numbered, starting at zero. So the first value is stored in element zero, the second value is stored in element 1, and so on.

Array elements start numbering at zero, not one.

An array is declared in the same way as other variables but additionally the size of the array should be specified in the declaration, in square brackets following the array name.

Optionally, an array can be initialized when it is declared by assigning values to each element as a comma-separated list enclosed by curly brackets (braces).

An individual element can be referenced using the array name followed by square brackets containing its element number.

This example creates an array of three elements and assigns initial values to them. The second element is then changed before each value is displayed in the program output.

array.cpp

```cpp
#include <iostream>
using namespace std;

int main()
{
    int arr[3] = { 100, 200, 300 };
    arr[1] = 555;           //change the middle element
    cout << "arr[0]: " << arr[0] << endl;
    cout << "arr[1]: " << arr[1] << endl;
    cout << "arr[2]: " << arr[2] << endl;
    return 0;
}
```

```
C:\ Command Prompt                              _ □ ✕

C:\MyPrograms>c++ array.cpp -o array.exe

C:\MyPrograms>array
arr[0]: 100
arr[1]: 555
arr[2]: 300
```

Character arrays

Arrays are not limited to the int data type but can be created for any C++ data type – int, float, double, bool, char. However, all the elements of an array must be of the same data type.

An array of characters, where each element stores a single character, can be used to store a string of text if the array's final element contains the special \0 null character. This allows the entire string to be referenced from just the array name.

This is demonstrated in the example below that retrieves a single character from a char array, then its entire string content:

arrays.cpp

Remember to allow an extra element to contain the \0 null character if you want to store strings in a char array.

```cpp
#include <iostream>
using namespace std;

int main()
{
    bool flags[3] = { true, true, false };
    double nums[3] = { 1.23, 4.56, 7.89 };
    char fname[5] = { 'm','i','k','e', '\0' };
    cout << flags[2] << endl;
    cout << nums[0] << endl;
    cout << fname[0] << endl;       //output character
    cout << fname << endl;          //output string
    return 0;
}
```

```
Command Prompt                          _ □ ✕
C:\MyPrograms>c++ arrays.cpp -o arrays.exe

C:\MyPrograms>arrays
0
1.23
m
mike

C:\MyPrograms>_
```

Character arrays are the principal means of working with strings in C but the C++ string class, introduced in Chapter 5, is simpler.

Multidimensional arrays

An array can have more than one index – to represent multiple dimensions, rather than the single dimension of a regular array. Multidimensional arrays of three indices and more are uncommon, but 2-dimensional arrays are useful to store grid-based information such as coordinates.

The following example creates a 2-dimensional array of two indexes, with three elements each. This represents a table of two rows, with three columns each. The first row, or index, contains numbers 1–3 and the second row, or index, contains numbers 4–6.

Notice the arrangement of the braces to assign initial values to each element of the indices in the array declaration:

array2d.cpp

```cpp
#include <iostream>
using namespace std;

int main()
{
    int arr[2][3] = { {1,2,3} , {4,5,6} };

    cout << "arr[0][0] contains " << arr[0][0] << endl;
    cout << "arr[0][1] contains " << arr[0][1] << endl;
    cout << "arr[0][2] contains " << arr[0][2] << endl;
    cout << "arr[1][0] contains " << arr[1][0] << endl;
    cout << "arr[1][1] contains " << arr[1][1] << endl;
    cout << "arr[1][2] contains " << arr[1][2] << endl;
    return 0;
}
```

Command Prompt

```
C:\MyPrograms>c++ array2d.cpp -o array2d.exe

C:\MyPrograms>array2d
arr[0][0] contains 1
arr[0][1] contains 2
arr[0][2] contains 3
arr[1][0] contains 4
arr[1][1] contains 5
arr[1][2] contains 6
```

Vectors

A vector is an alternative to a regular array and has the advantage that its size can be changed as the program requires. Like regular arrays, vectors can be created for any data type and their elements are numbered starting at zero.

In order to use vectors in a program the C++ <vector> library must be added with an #include directive at the start of the program. This library contains the predefined methods in the table below which are used to work with vectors:

at(*element-number*)	gets the value contained in the specified element
back()	gets the value in the final element
clear()	erases the vector
empty()	returns true (1) if the vector is empty, or false (0) otherwise
front()	gets the value in the first element
pop_back()	removes the final element
push_back(*value*)	adds an element to the end of the vector, containing the specified value
size()	gets the number of elements

A declaration to create a vector has this syntax:

```
vector < data-type > vector-name ( size ) ;
```

An int vector will by default have each of its elements initialized with a value of zero. Optionally a different initial value can be specified in the declaration after the size using the syntax:

```
vector < data-type > vector-name ( size , value ) ;
```

The methods to work with vectors are simply appended to the given vector name by the dot operator, vector-name.method(). The program on the opposite page demonstrates how each of the methods listed above is used to manipulate vector elements.

vector.cpp

```cpp
#include <iostream>
#include <vector>
using namespace std;

int main()
{
  vector <int> vec(3,100);
  cout << "Vector size is " << vec.size() << endl;
  vec.push_back(7); vec.push_back(8); vec.push_back(9);
  cout << "\t3 elements added"  << endl;
  cout << "Vector size is now " << vec.size() << endl;
  cout << "\tFirst element is "<< vec.front() << endl;
  cout << "\tSecond element is "<< vec.at(1)  << endl;
  cout << "\tLast element is " << vec.back()  << endl;
  vec.pop_back();
  cout << "\tLast element removed" << endl;
  cout << "\tLast element is now " <<vec.back() <<endl;
  cout << "Vector size is now "    <<vec.size() <<endl;
  cout << "Is vector empty?: "     << vec.empty()<<endl;
  vec.clear();
  cout << "\tVector cleared"    << endl;
  cout << "Vector size is now " << vec.size() << endl;
  cout << "Is vector empty?: "  << vec.empty() << endl;
  return 0;
}
```

Single vector elements can be addressed by their index number in square brackets, just like array elements.

The example on page 52 shows how to use a loop to populate a vector with different initial values in each element.

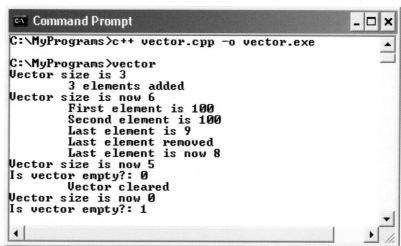

```
C:\MyPrograms>c++ vector.cpp -o vector.exe

C:\MyPrograms>vector
Vector size is 3
        3 elements added
Vector size is now 6
        First element is 100
        Second element is 100
        Last element is 9
        Last element removed
        Last element is now 8
Vector size is now 5
Is vector empty?: 0
        Vector cleared
Vector size is now 0
Is vector empty?: 1
```

Constants

Data that will not change during the execution of a program should be stored in a constant container, rather than in a variable. This better enables the compiler to check the code for errors – if the program attempts to change the value stored in a constant the compiler will report an error and the compilation will fail.

Use uppercase for constant names – to differentiate them from lowercase variable names.

A constant can be created for any data type by prefixing the declaration with the const keyword, followed by a space. Unlike variables, constants must always be initialized on declaration.

The program below creates a constant for the mathematical value of pi. This is a fixed value that should never be changed so there is no need to store it in a variable container. It is good programming practice to use constants wherever possible.

constant.cpp

```cpp
#include <iostream>
using namespace std;

int main()
{
   const double PI = 3.14159;
   double rad;

   cout << "Enter the radius of a circle: ";
   cin >> rad;
   cout << "Diameter: " << ( rad + rad ) << endl;
   cout << "Area: " << (PI *( rad * rad) ) << endl;
   cout << "Circumference: " << (PI *(rad+rad)) << endl;
   return 0;
}
```

The asterisk character in this example is the C++ arithmetical multiplication operator.

```
Command Prompt                                      _ □ ✕

C:\MyPrograms>c++ constant.cpp -o constant.exe

C:\MyPrograms>constant
Enter the radius of a circle: 10
Diameter: 20
Area: 314.159
Circumference: 62.8318

C:\MyPrograms>_
```

Enumerating constants

The enum keyword provides a handy way to create a sequence of integer constants in a concise manner. Optionally the declaration can include a name for the sequence after the enum keyword. The constant names follow as a comma-separated list within braces.

Notice how parentheses have been used to bracket the arithmetical expressions in the examples on both these pages.

Each of the constants will by default have a value 1 greater than the constant that it follows in the list. Unless specified the first constant will have a value of zero, the next a value of 1, and so on. The constants can be assigned any individual value but the following constants will always increment it one by one.

This example represents the points value of balls in the game of snooker starting at 1 for a red ball, right up to 7 for the black ball. The sequence is named "balls" but this could have been omitted.

enum.cpp

```
#include <iostream>
using namespace std;

int main()
{
  enum balls{RED=1,YELLOW,GREEN,BROWN,BLUE,PINK,BLACK};
  int total;

  cout << "I potted a red worth "<< RED << endl;
  cout << "Then a black worth " << BLACK << endl;
  cout << "Followed by another red worth "<< RED<<endl;
  total = (RED + BLACK + RED);
  cout << "Altogether I scored " << total << endl;
  return 0;
}
```

Assigning a value of 1 to the BLUE constant in this example would automatically make the PINK constant 2 and the BLACK constant 3.

```
C:\MyPrograms>c++ enum.cpp -o enum.exe

C:\MyPrograms>enum
I potted a red worth 1
Then a black worth 7
Followed by another red worth 1
Altogether I scored 9

C:\MyPrograms>_
```

Creating a constant type

If a program uses a number of variables of the same data type and qualifier it is sometimes convenient to create a constant to represent that type to act as a kind of shorthand. For instance, it could become tedious to repeatedly have to write unsigned short int so a constant may be created with the typedef keyword to represent that type. Its declaration should appear at the start of the program, right after the preprocessor directives. The syntax to declare a constant name for a type looks like this:

```
typedef data-type NAME ;
```

This usefully creates a synonym for the data type that can be used in the program anywhere that the lengthy version might appear. The example below creates a constant named USHRT to represent the unsigned short int data type:

typedef.cpp

This process does not create a new type – merely a short nickname for the specified type.

```cpp
#include <iostream>
using namespace std;

typedef unsigned short int USHRT;

int main()
{
  USHRT width;
  USHRT length;
  cout << "Enter width: ";   cin >> width;
  cout << "Enter length: ";  cin >> length;
  cout << "Area is " << width * length << endl;
  return 0;
}
```

```
Command Prompt
C:\MyPrograms>c++ typedef.cpp -o typedef.exe

C:\MyPrograms>typedef
Enter width: 5
Enter length: 10
Area is 50
```

Defining constants

The preprocessor directive #define can be used to specify constant text values that can be used in the program with this syntax:

```
#define CONSTANT-NAME "text-string"
```

This technique is only given for completeness because you may find it in existing program code. The creation of constants with the const keyword provides better type checking so that technique should be used in all new program code.

Like the #include directive, these should appear at the very start of the program code. Any occurrences of the specified constant name in the program code has its associated text string substituted by the compiler before the program is compiled.

The example below defines three string constants with #define preprocessor directives and their specified constant names are used in the calls to the cout function. When this program is compiled the text strings are substituted in place of the constant names.

define.cpp

```
#include <iostream>
using namespace std;
#define LINE   "_____"
#define TITLE "C++ Programming in easy steps"
#define AUTHOR "Mike McGrath"
#define TAB "\t"

int main()
{
  cout << TAB << LINE   << endl;
  cout << TAB << TITLE  << endl;
  cout << TAB << "by " << AUTHOR << endl;
  cout << TAB << LINE   << endl;
  return 0;
}
```

The LINE string in this example is just a series of underscore characters.

```
C:\MyPrograms>c++ define.cpp -o define.exe

C:\MyPrograms>define

        C++ Programming in easy steps
        by Mike McGrath
```

Converting data types

Any data stored in a variable can be forced (coerced) into a variable of a different data type by a process known as "casting". A cast just states the data type to which the value should be converted in plain brackets before its variable name, like this:

```
variable-name = ( data-type ) variable-name ;
```

The example below casts float, char, double and bool data type values into int type variables:

cast.cpp

```cpp
#include <iostream>
using namespace std;

int main()
{
    int num1, num2, num3, num4;    //int variables
    float decimal = 7.75;          //non-int variables
    char letter = 'A';
    double precise = 123.987654;
    bool flag = true;

    num1 = (int) decimal;          //cast values to int
    num2 = (int) letter;
    num3 = (int) precise;
    num4 = (int) flag;

    cout << "num1: " << num1 << endl;
    cout << "num2: " << num2 << endl;
    cout << "num3: " << num3 << endl;
    cout << "num4: " << num4 << endl;
    return 0;
}
```

"ASCII" (pronounced "as-kee") stands for "American Standard Code for Information Interchange" and is the accepted standard for plain text. Characters are represented by a numerical ASCII code within the range of 0–127. The uppercase letter "A" in this example is represented by the ASCII numerical code of 65, so that is its integer value when cast into an int type variable.

```
Command Prompt                                    _ □ ✕
C:\MyPrograms>c++ cast.cpp -o cast.exe

C:\MyPrograms>cast
num1: 7
num2: 65
num3: 123
num4: 1
```

Performing operations

All the common C++ language operators are detailed in this chapter which illustrates, by example, how to perform arithmetical operations, how to assign values and how to make comparisons. The logical operators are explained and demonstrated, too, along with the conditional operator.

Covers

Chapter Three

Arithmetical operators

The arithmetical operators commonly used in C++ programs are listed in the table below together with the operation they perform:

Operator	Operation
+	Addition
-	Subtraction
*	Multiplication
/	Division
%	Modulus
++	Increment
--	Decrement

The numbers used along with operators to form expressions are called "operands" – in the expression 2 + 3 the numbers 2 and 3 are the operands.

The operators for addition, subtraction, multiplication and division act as you would expect. Care must be taken, however, to bracket expressions where more than one of these operators is used, to clarify the expression.

```
a = b * c - d % e / f ;           // this is unclear

a = (b * c) - ((d % e) / f );     // this is clearer
```

The % modulus operator will divide the first given number by the second given number and return the remainder of the operation. This is useful to determine if a number has an odd or even value.

The ++ increment operator and – – decrement operator alter the given value by 1 and return the resulting new value. These are most commonly used to count iterations in a loop. The ++ increment operator increases the value by one while the – – decrement operator decreases the value by one.

The increment and decrement operators can be placed before or after a value, to different effect. If placed before the operand (prefix), its value is immediately changed, if placed after the operand (postfix) its value is noted first, then the value is changed.

The difference between placing the increment operator before and after an int variable operand is demonstrated in this example which illustrates each of the arithmetical operators in action:

arithmetic.cpp

```cpp
#include <iostream>
using namespace std;

int main()
{
    int a = 4, b = 8, c = 1, d = 1, result;

    result = a + b;   //4 + 8
    cout << "Added numbers total " << result << endl;
    result = b - a;   //8 - 4
    cout << "Subtracted numbers total " << result<< endl;
    result = a * b;   //4 * 8
    cout << "Multiplied numbers total " << result<< endl;
    result = b / a;   //8 / 4
    cout << "Divided numbers total " << result << endl;
    result = b % a;   //8 % 4
    cout << "Modulus of numbers is " << result << endl;

    cout << "Postfix increment is " << c++ << endl;
    cout << "Now postfix increment is " << c << endl;
    cout << "Prefix increment is " << ++d << endl;
    cout << "Now prefix increment is " << d << endl;
    return 0;
}
```

Remember that the prefix operator increments the variable value immediately – the postfix operator only increments its value subsequently.

```
C:\MyPrograms>c++ arithmetic.cpp -o arithmetic.exe

C:\MyPrograms>arithmetic
Added numbers total 12
Subtracted numbers total 4
Multiplied numbers total 32
Divided numbers total 2
Modulus of numbers is 0
Postfix increment is 1
Now postfix increment is 2
Prefix increment is 2
Now prefix increment is 2
```

Logical operators

The logical operators most commonly used in C++ programs are listed in the table below:

Operator	Operation
&&	Logical AND
||	Logical OR
!	Logical NOT

The logical operators are used with operands that have the boolean values of true or false, or are values that convert to true or false.

The logical && AND operator will evaluate two operands and return true only if both operands themselves are true. Otherwise the && operator will return false.

This is used in conditional branching where the direction of a C++ program is determined by testing two conditions. If both conditions are satisfied the program will go in a certain direction, otherwise it will take a different direction.

Unlike the && operator that needs both operands to be true the || OR operator will evaluate its two operands and return true if either one of the operands itself returns true. If neither operand returns true then || will return false. This is useful in C++ programming to perform a certain action if either one of two test conditions has been met.

The third logical operator ! NOT is a unary operator that is used before a single operand. It returns the inverse value of the given operand so if the variable a had a value of true then !a would have a value of false. The ! operator is useful in C++ programs to toggle the value of a variable in successive loop iterations with a statement like a=!a. This ensures that on each pass the value is changed, like flicking a light switch on and off.

In C++ programs a zero represents the boolean false value and any non-zero value, such as 1, represents the boolean true value.

The term "boolean" refers to a system of logical thought developed by the English mathematician George Boole (1815–64).

Where there is more than one operand the expression must be surrounded by parentheses.

The example below demonstrates how boolean values can be tested with each of the logical operators shown opposite. The ! NOT operator reverses the boolean value, && AND returns 1 if both operands are non-zero values and || OR returns 1 if either operand is a non-zero value.

logic.cpp

```cpp
#include <iostream>
using namespace std;

int main()
{
    int a = 1, b = 0;
    cout << "a = " << a << "\tb = " << b << endl;
    cout << "AND examples:" << endl;
    cout << "\t a && a = " << (a && a) << " (true)\n";
    cout << "\t a && b = " << (a && b) << " (false)\n";
    cout << "\t b && b = " << (b && b) << " (false)\n";
    cout << "OR examples:" << endl;
    cout << "\t a || a = " << (a || a) << " (true)\n";
    cout << "\t a || b = " << (a || b) << " (true)\n";
    cout << "\t b || b = " << (b || b) << " (false)\n";
    cout << "NOT examples:" << endl;
    cout << "\t a = " << a << " !a = " << !a << endl;
    cout << "\t b = " << b << " !b = " << !b << endl;
    return 0;
}
```

Notice that 0 && 0 returns 0, not 1 – demonstrating the maxim "two wrongs don't make a right".

```
C:\MyPrograms>c++ logic.cpp -o logic.exe

C:\MyPrograms>logic
a = 1    b = 0
AND examples:
        a && a = 1 (true)
        a && b = 0 (false)
        b && b = 0 (false)
OR examples:
        a || a = 1 (true)
        a || b = 1 (true)
        b || b = 0 (false)
NOT examples:
        a = 1  !a = 0
        b = 0  !b = 1
```

Assignment operators

The operators that are used in C++ programming to assign values are listed in the table below. All except the simple = assign operator are a shorthand form of a longer expression so each equivalent is also given for clarity.

Operator	Example	Equivalent
=	a = b	a = b
+=	a += b	a = (a + b)
–=	a –= b	a = (a – b)
*=	a *= b	a = (a * b)
/=	a /= b	a = (a / b)
%=	a %= b	a = (a % b)

The == equality operator compares operand values and is described on page 40.

It is important to regard the = operator to mean "assign" rather than "equals" to avoid confusion with the == equality operator.

In the example above the variable named a is assigned the value that is contained in the variable named b – so that becomes the new value stored in the a variable.

The += operator is useful to add a value onto an existing value that is stored in a variable.

In the table example the += operator first adds the value contained in variable a to the value contained in the variable named b. It then assigns the result to become the new value stored in the a variable.

All the other operators in the table work in the same way by making the arithmetical operation between the two values first, then assigning the result to the first variable to become its new stored value.

With the %= operator the first operand a is divided by the second operand b then the remainder of the operation is assigned to the a variable.

The example program below performs a series of operations to demonstrate each of the assignment operators in action:

assign.cpp

```cpp
#include <iostream>
using namespace std;

int main()
{
  int a, b;

  cout << "Assign values example:";
  cout << "\n\tVariable a = " << (a = 8);
  cout << "\n\tVariable b = " << (b = 4);

  cout << "\nAdd & assign example:\n";
  cout << "\tVariable a += b (8 += 4) a = " <<(a += b);
  cout << "\nSubtract & assign example:\n";
  cout << "\tVariable a -= b (12 -= 4) a = "<<(a -= b);
  cout << "\nMultiply & assign example:\n";
  cout << "\tVariable a *= b (8 *= 4) a = " <<(a *= b);
  cout << "\nDivide & assign example:\n";
  cout << "\tVariable a /= b (32 /= 4) a = "<<(a /= b);
  cout << "\nModulus & assign example:\n";
  cout << "\tVariable a %= b (8 %= 4) a = " <<(a %= b);
  return 0;
}
```

```
Command Prompt                                    _ □ X
C:\MyPrograms>c++ assign.cpp -o assign.exe

C:\MyPrograms>assign
Assign values example:
        Variable a = 8
        Variable b = 4
Add & assign example:
        Variable a += b (8 += 4) a = 12
Subtract & assign example:
        Variable a -= b (12 -= 4) a = 8
Multiply & assign example:
        Variable a *= b (8 *= 4) a = 32
Divide & assign example:
        Variable a /= b (32 /= 4) a = 8
Modulus & assign example:
        Variable a %= b (8 %= 4) a = 0
```

Comparison operators

The operators that are commonly used in C++ programming to compare two numerical values are listed in the table below:

Operator	Comparative Test
==	Equality
!=	Inequality
>	Greater than
<	Less than
>=	Greater than or equal to
<=	Less than or equal to

The A–Z uppercase characters have ASCII codes 65–90 and a–z lowercase characters have ASCII codes 97–122.

The == equality operator compares two operands and will return 1 (true) if both are equal in value, otherwise it will return 0 (false). If both are the same number they are equal, or if both are characters their ASCII code value is compared numerically.

Conversely the != inequality operator returns 1 (true) if two operands are not equal, using the same rules as the == equality operator, otherwise it returns 0 (false).

Equality and inequality operators are useful in testing the state of two variables to perform conditional branching in a program.

The > "greater than" operator compares two operands and will return 1 (true) if the first is greater in value than the second, or it will return 0 (false) if it is equal or less in value. The > "greater than" operator is frequently used to test the value of a countdown value in a loop. The < "less than" operators makes the same comparison but returns 1 (true) if the first operand is less in value than the second, otherwise it returns 0 (false).

Adding the = operator after a > "greater than" or < "less than" operator makes it also return true if the two operands are exactly equal in value. The example program on the opposite page demonstrates each comparison operator in action.

comparison.cpp

The ASCII code value for uppercase "A" is 65 and for lowercase "a" it's 97 – so their comparison in this example returns 0 (false).

```cpp
#include <iostream>
using namespace std;

int main()
{
  int zero = 0, nil = 0, one = 1;
  char lg = 'A', sm = 'a' ;

  cout << "Equality example:\n";
  cout << "\tIs zero equal to nil? " << (zero == nil);
  cout << "\tIs large equal to small? " << (lg == sm);
  cout << "Inequality example:\n";
  cout << "\tIs zero not equal to one?"<<(zero != one);
  cout << "Greater than example:\n";
  cout << "\tIs zero greater than one? "<<(zero > one);
  cout << "Less than example:\n";
  cout << "\tIs zero less than one? " << (zero < one);
  cout << "Greater than or equal to example:\n";
  cout << "\tIs zero greater than or equal to nil? ";
  cout << (zero >= nil);
  cout << "Less than or equal to example:\n";
  cout << "\tIs one less than or equal to nil? ";
  cout << (one <= nil);
  return 0;
}
```

```
C:\MyPrograms>c++ comparison.cpp -o comparison.exe

C:\MyPrograms>comparison
Equality example:
        Is zero equal to nil? 1 (true)
        Is large equal to small? 0 (false)
Inequality example:
        Is zero not equal to one? 1 (true)
Greater than example:
        Is zero greater than one? 0 (false)
Less than example:
        Is zero less than one? 1 (true)
Greater than or equal to example:
        Is zero more than or equal to nil? 1 (true)
Less than or equal to example:
        Is one less than or equal to nil? 0 (false)
```

Conditional operator

Possibly the C++ programmer's favorite test operator is the ?: "conditional" operator. This operator first evaluates an expression for a true or false value then executes one of two given statements depending on the result of the evaluation.

The conditional operator has this syntax:

```
(test-expression) ? if-true-do-this : if-false-do-this;
```

This operator is used to execute program statements according to the result of its conditional test. The example below evaluates two integer variable values to determine if they are odd or even numbers. The program outputs an appropriate message according to the result of the test.

conditional.cpp

In this example the first two instances of the conditional operator execute the appropriate cout function call, whereas the final conditional test assigns the relevant character value to the char letter variable.

```cpp
#include <iostream>
using namespace std;

int main()
{
  int num1 = 13579, num2 = 24680;
  char letter;

  cout << num1 << " is ";
  (num1 %2 != 0) ? cout << "odd" : cout << "even";

  cout << endl << num2 << " is ";
  (num2 %2 != 0) ? cout << "odd" : cout << "even";

  letter = (num2 %2 != 0) ? 'Y' : 'N';
  cout << "\nIs " << num2 << " odd?: " << letter;
  return 0;
}
```

```
Command Prompt                                    _ □ ✕

C:\MyPrograms>c++ conditional.cpp -o conditional.ex

C:\MyPrograms>conditional
13579 is odd
24680 is even
Is 24680 odd?: N
C:\MyPrograms>_
```

Sizeof operator

The sizeof operator returns an integer value that is the number of bytes needed to store the contents of its operand. The operand can be a data type contained inside parentheses or an expression without parentheses. Both techniques appear in this example which uses the sizeof operator to ascertain the size, in bytes, of all the standard data types, a variable and two arrays:

sizeofop.cpp

```cpp
#include <iostream>
using namespace std;

int main()
{
  float num = 98.6;
  int ints[50];
  char chars[50];

  cout << "int: "    << sizeof(int)    << " bytes\n";
  cout << "float: "  << sizeof(float)  << " bytes\n";
  cout << "double: " << sizeof(double) << " bytes\n";
  cout << "char: "   << sizeof(char)   << " bytes\n";
  cout << "bool: "   << sizeof(bool)   << " bytes\n";

  cout << "float variable: ";
  cout << (sizeof num) << " bytes\n";
  cout << "50 float array:"<< (sizeof ints) <<" bytes\n";
  cout << "50 char array:"<<(sizeof chars) <<" bytes\n";
  return 0;
}
```

The number of bytes allocated to data types is implementation-dependent – so this program's output may be different on your system.

```
C:\MyPrograms>c++ sizeofop.cpp -o sizeofop.exe

C:\MyPrograms>sizeofop
int: 4 bytes
float: 4 bytes
double: 8 bytes
char: 1 bytes
bool: 1 bytes
float variable: 4 bytes
50 float array: 200 bytes
50 char array: 50 bytes

C:\MyPrograms>_
```

Operator precedence

Operator precedence defines the order in which C++ evaluates expressions. For instance, in the expression a=6+b*3, the order of precedence determines whether the addition or the multiplication is completed first. The table below gives the precedence in decreasing order – operators on the top row have the highest precedence, those on lower rows have successively lower precedence Operators on the same row have equal precedence.

Operator		Associativity
( ) (function call) [ ] (array index) –> (class pointer) . (class member)		Left to right
! (logical NOT) sizeof (sizeof) ++ (increment) - - (decrement) + (positive sign) – (negative sign) * (pointer) & (addressof)		Right to left
* (multiply) / (divide) % (modulus)		Left to right
+ (add) – (subtract)		Left to right
< (less than) <= (less or equal) > (greater than) >= (greater or equal		Left to right
== (equality) != (inequality)		Left to right
&& (logical AND)		Left to right
|| (logical OR)		Left to right
? : (conditional)		Right to left
= += –= *= /= %= (assignments)		Right to left
, (comma)		Left to right

In addition to the operators listed above there are a number of "bitwise" operators which are used to perform binary arithmetic. This is outside the scope of this book but there is a chapter devoted to binary arithmetic in "C Programming in easy steps". The bitwise operators described there perform just the same in C++.

Making statements

Statements are used in C++ programming to progress the execution of a program. They may define loops within the code or state expressions to be evaluated. This chapter demonstrates conditional testing and illustrates different kinds of loop.

Covers

Chapter Four

Conditional if statement

The if keyword is used to perform the basic conditional test that evaluates a given expression for a boolean value of true or false. Statements following the evaluation will only be executed when the expression is found to be true.

The syntax for the if statement looks like this:

```
if (test-expression) { code-to-be-executed-when-true }
```

When the code to be executed is just a single statement the braces may, optionally, be omitted.

The code to be executed may be multiple statements, all contained within the braces, each ending with a semi-colon.

In the example program below the test expression evaluates whether one number is greater than another. If the first number is, in fact, greater than the second number the expression will be true so the statements inside the braces following the test will be executed. If the expression was false the statements following the test would not be executed and the program would just move on to the next test, or statement, in the code.

iftest.cpp

The test expression in this example could alternatively be if(1 < 5) – is 1 less than 5?

```cpp
#include <iostream>
using namespace std;

int main()
{
  if( 5 > 1 )
  {
    cout << "Yes, 5 is greater than 1\n";
    cout << "Thanks for asking\n";
  }
  return 0;
}
```

```
Command Prompt                                    _ □ ✕

C:\MyPrograms>c++ iftest.cpp -o iftest.exe

C:\MyPrograms>iftest
Yes, 5 is greater than 1
Thanks for asking

C:\MyPrograms>_
```

Nesting if statements

Conditional if statements can be nested inside other if statement blocks to test multiple expressions. In this example the three statements calling the cout function will only be executed when all three tested expressions are true.

ifnest.cpp

```cpp
#include <iostream>
using namespace std;

int main()
{
  if( 5 > 1 )
  {
    if('A' == 'A')
    {
      if( 1 != 0 )
      {
          cout << "Yes, 5 is greater than 1\n";
          cout << "and A is equal to A\n";
          cout << "and 1 does not equal 0\n";
      }
    }
  }
  return 0;
}
```

Be sure to use the == equality operator to test for equality, rather than the = assignment operator.

```
Command Prompt                                    - □ ×
C:\MyPrograms>c++ ifnest.cpp -o ifnest.exe

C:\MyPrograms>ifnest
Yes, 5 is greater than 1
and A is equal to A
and 1 does not equal 0
```

When testing multiple expressions enclose each expression inside parentheses.

An alternative method to evaluate multiple expressions with an if statement employs the && logical AND operator. The evaluations in the program listed above could be made in a single test like this:

```cpp
if( ( 5 > 1 ) && ( 'A'=='A' ) && ( 1 != 0 ) ) { ..... }
```

If-else statement block

The else keyword can be used with an if statement to specify alternative code to be executed when the test expression is false. This is known as "conditional branching" because the program will branch along a certain route according to the result of a test. The syntax of an if-else statement looks like this:

```
if (test-expression){do-this-if-true} else { do-this }
```

Several expressions can be tested using successive else statements until a true value is found – whereupon its associated statements will be executed. This example illustrates how the if-else statement ends after the statements in a single true test have been executed:

ifelse.cpp

```cpp
#include <iostream>
using namespace std;

int main()
{
  int num = 2; bool flag = 0;
  if( (num == 2) && (flag) )
  {
    cout << "The first test is true\n";
  }
  else if( (num == 2) && (!flag) )
  {
    cout << "The second test is true\n";
  }
  else if( (num == 2) && (flag == 0) )
  {
    cout << "The third test is true - but unreached\n";
  }
  return 0;
}
```

This example uses shorthand for boolean values – (bool) is true shorthand for (bool == 1) and (!bool) is false shorthand for (bool == 0).

```
Command Prompt                                    _ □ ✕
C:\MyPrograms>c++ ifelse.cpp -o ifelse.exe

C:\MyPrograms>ifelse
The second test is true

C:\MyPrograms>_
```

The switch statement

Conditional branching with long if-else statements can often be more efficiently performed using a switch statement instead, especially when the test expression just evaluates a single integer.

Each character is represented by the integer value of its ASCII code.

The switch statement works in an unusual way. It takes a given integer value then seeks a matching value among a number of case statements. Code associated with the matching case statement will be executed or default code may execute if no match is found. Each case statement must end with a break statement to prevent the program continuing through the switch block.

This program gets a single character value from the user then executes the appropriate case statement code:

switch.cpp

```cpp
#include <iostream>
using namespace std;

int main()
{
  char letter;

  cout << "Enter any  a-z character: ";
  cin >> letter;

  switch(letter)
  {
    case 'a' : cout << "Letter \'a\' found\n"; break;
    case 'b' : cout << "Letter \'b\' found\n"; break;
    case 'c' : cout << "Letter \'c\' found\n"; break;
    default  : cout << "Letter is not a, b or c\n";
  }
  return 0;
}
```

Quotes nested within other quotes must be escaped with the backslash character to avoid confusing the compiler.

```
C:\ Command Prompt                                _ □ ×

C:\MyPrograms>c++ switch.cpp -o switch.exe

C:\MyPrograms>switch
Enter any  a-z character: b
Letter 'b' found
```

For loops

A loop is a piece of code in a program that automatically repeats. One complete execution of all the statements within a loop is called an "iteration" or "pass".

The length of a loop is controlled by a conditional test made within the loop. While the tested expression is true the loop will continue – until the test-expression is found to be false when the loop ends.

In C++ there are three types of loop: for loops, while loops and do-while loops. Perhaps the most common of these is the for loop, which has this syntax:

```
for(initializer; test-expression; increment){statements}
```

The initializer is used to set a starting value for a counter of the number of iterations made by the loop. An integer variable is used for this purpose and is traditionally named "i".

Alternatively, a for loop counter can count downwards by decrementing the counter value on each pass using i-- instead of i++.

Upon each iteration of the loop the test-expression is evaluated and that iteration will only continue while this expression is true. When the test-expression becomes false the loop ends immediately without executing the statements again. With every iteration the counter is incremented then the loop's statements are executed.

The example below demonstrates a for loop that outputs the number of the current iteration on each pass. When the counter reaches 3 the test-expression becomes false so the loop is terminated. The output is illustrated on the next page together with a further example showing how for loops can be nested.

forloop.cpp

```cpp
#include <iostream>
using namespace std;

int main()
{
  int i;
  for(i = 0; i < 3; i++)
  {
      cout << "For loop iteration " << i << endl;
  }
  return 0;
}
```

```
C:\ Command Prompt                                    _ □ ✕
C:\MyPrograms>c++ forloop.cpp -o forloop.exe          ▲

C:\MyPrograms>forloop
For loop iteration 0
For loop iteration 1
For loop iteration 2                                  ▼
◄                                                    ►
```

fornest.cpp

```cpp
#include <iostream>
using namespace std;

int main()
{
  int i, j;

  for(i = 1; i < 4; i++)
  {
    cout << "Outer loop iteration " << i << endl;
    for(j = 1; j < 4; j++)
    {
      cout << "\tInner loop iteration " << j << endl;
    }
  }
  return 0;
}
```

```
C:\ Command Prompt                                    _ □ ✕
C:\MyPrograms>c++ fornest.cpp -o fornest.exe          ▲

C:\MyPrograms>fornest
Outer loop iteration 1
        Inner loop iteration 1
        Inner loop iteration 2
        Inner loop iteration 3
Outer loop iteration 2
        Inner loop iteration 1
        Inner loop iteration 2
        Inner loop iteration 3
Outer loop iteration 3
        Inner loop iteration 1
        Inner loop iteration 2
        Inner loop iteration 3                        ▼
◄                                                    ►
```

While loops

Another type of loop uses the while keyword followed by an expression to be evaluated for a true or false value. If the expression is found to be true then the statements contained within braces following the tested expression will be executed. After the statements have all been executed the test-expression will again be evaluated and the loop will continue until the test-expression is found to be false.

The loop's statement block must contain code that will affect the test-expression in order to change the evaluation result to false, otherwise an infinite loop is created that will lock the system. Note that if the test-expression is found to be false when it is first evaluated the code in the statement block is never executed.

This example fills a vector and displays each element value:

while.cpp

```cpp
#include <vector>
#include <iostream>
using namespace std;

int main()
{
  vector <int> vec(18);
  int i = 0;
  while( i < vec.size() )
  {
    vec[i] = (i + 1);              //populate values 1-18
    cout << " " << vec.at(i);      //display each element
    i++;
  }
  cout << endl;
  return 0;
}
```

For more on vectors see page 26.

```
Command Prompt                                       _ □ ✕

C:\MyPrograms>c++ while.cpp -o while.exe

C:\MyPrograms>while
 1 2 3 4 5 6 7 8 9 10 11 12 13 14 15 16 17 18

C:\MyPrograms>_
```

The do-while loop

The do-while loop is a subtle variation of the while loop described on the opposite page. In this loop the do keyword is followed by a statement block within braces containing all the statements to be executed on each iteration.

A while loop is often more suitable than a do-while loop because its statements are not automatically executed on the first iteration.

The statement block is then followed by the while keyword and an expression to be evaluated for a true or false value. If the expression is true the loop continues from the do keyword until the test-expression is found to be false – whereupon the loop ends.

Note that, unlike the while loop, the statements in the do-while loop's statement block will always be executed at least once because the test-expression is not tried until the end of the loop.

The following example will never loop because the counter value is incremented to 1 in the very first execution of the statement block – so the test-expression is found to be false at the first test.

dowhile.cpp

```
#include <iostream>
using namespace std;

int main()
{
    int a = 0, i = 0;

    do
    {
    ++a; ++i; cout << "Variable a is " << a << endl;
    }
    while( i < 1 );

    return 0;
}
```

Changing the (i < 1) test to (i > 0) in this example will create an infinite loop. In this case press the Ctrl+C keyboard keys to halt the program.

```
Command Prompt                              _ □ ✕

C:\MyPrograms>c++ dowhile.cpp -o dowhile.exe

C:\MyPrograms>dowhile
Variable a is 1

C:\MyPrograms>_
```

Break and continue statements

The break keyword was introduced on page 49 to exit individual case statements inside a switch statement. It has a further important use, however, to exit from any loop.

A break statement can be included inside any loop statement block, preceded by a conditional test. When that test is found to be true the break statement immediately terminates the loop and no further iterations will be made.

In the following example a while loop is set to complete 10 iterations, but when the counter reaches 7 the break statement terminates the loop at once.

dobreak.cpp

```cpp
#include <iostream>
using namespace std;

int main()
{
  int i = 0;

  while( i < 10 )
  {
    ++i;
    cout << "Loop iteration is " << i ;
    //if the counter hits 7 exit the loop...
    if(i == 7) break;
    cout << " - go to the next pass\n";
  }
  return 0;
}
```

A break statement stops a loop instantly – no further iterations are made.

```
Command Prompt                                    _ □ ✕

C:\MyPrograms>c++ dobreak.cpp -o dobreak.exe

C:\MyPrograms>dobreak
Loop iteration is 1 - go to the next pass
Loop iteration is 2 - go to the next pass
Loop iteration is 3 - go to the next pass
Loop iteration is 4 - go to the next pass
Loop iteration is 5 - go to the next pass
Loop iteration is 6 - go to the next pass
Loop iteration is 7
C:\MyPrograms>_
```

The C++ continue keyword can be used to interrupt the execution of a loop but has one important difference to the break keyword described opposite – the continue keyword only stops the execution of the current iteration of a loop.

Just like in a break statement, the continue keyword is preceded by a conditional test within the loop's statement block. When its test-expression is found to be true the current iteration is terminated immediately and the next iteration then begins. Note that the loop counter must be changed before a continue test-expression is encountered to avoid creating an infinite loop.

In the following example the test-expression is found to be true when the counter value reaches 3 – so that iteration of the loop is skipped but the loop continues to complete its other passes:

continue.cpp

```cpp
#include <iostream>
using namespace std;

int main()
{
    int i = 0;
    while(i < 6)
    {
        ++i;
        if(i == 3) continue;  //skip this pass
        cout << "Loop iteration is " << i ;
        cout << " - go to the next pass\n";
    }
    return 0;
}
```

```
Command Prompt                                    _ □ ✕
C:\MyPrograms>c++ continue.cpp -o continue.exe

C:\MyPrograms>continue
Loop iteration is 1 - go to the next pass
Loop iteration is 2 - go to the next pass
Loop iteration is 4 - go to the next pass
Loop iteration is 5 - go to the next pass
Loop iteration is 6 - go to the next pass
```

The infamous goto statement

The goto keyword supposedly allows the program flow to jump to labels at other points in the program, much like a hyperlink on a Web page. However, since in reality this can cause errors, its use is much-frowned upon and considered bad programming practice.

One possible valid use of the goto keyword is to break cleanly from a nested loop. This is shown in the example below which instantly exits both nested loops in the example listed on page 51.

On the whole, though, it should not be used and no other example in this book features the hapless goto keyword.

dogoto.cpp

The goto keyword has existed in computer programs for decades. Its power was abused by many early programmers who created programs that jumped around in an unfathomable manner. This created unreadable programs so the use of goto became hugely unpopular, and this remains so today.

```cpp
#include <iostream>
using namespace std;

int main()
{
  int i, j;

  for(i = 1; i < 4; i++)
  {
    cout << "Outer loop iteration " << i << endl;
    for(j = 1; j < 4; j++)
    {
      if(j == 3) goto end;        //jump to label
      cout << "\tInner loop iteration " << j << endl;
    }
  }
  end:                            //label
  return 0;
}
```

```
Command Prompt                                    _ □ ✕

C:\MyPrograms>c++ dogoto.cpp -o dogoto.exe

C:\MyPrograms>dogoto
Outer loop iteration 1
        Inner loop iteration 1
        Inner loop iteration 2

C:\MyPrograms>_
```

Working with strings

This chapter introduces the C++ <string> class that provides methods for handling text strings. These offer a simpler, more powerful, alternative to working with character arrays of text. The examples in this chapter demonstrate many useful ways to manipulate strings.

Covers

Chapter Five

A string variable

The C++ <string> class provides methods to manipulate strings of text. To make these available in a program the class must be added with an #include directive at the beginning of the code.

Once included in a program the <string> class allows a string data type variable to be declared that can be used to store text strings.

A string variable may be declared then initialized later by assignation of a text string using the = assignment operator. Alternatively there are two ways to initialize a string variable in its declaration: assign a value with the assignment operator, as usual, or include the string in parentheses after the variable's name.

The example below illustrates all of these techniques:

string.cpp

Strings of characters must always be surrounded by double quotes.

```cpp
#include <string>
#include <iostream>
using namespace std;

int main()
{
  string str1("Hello from C++");
  string str2 = "Programming in easy steps";
  string str3;

  str3 = "by Mike McGrath ";

  cout << "str1: " << str1 << endl;
  cout << "str2: " << str2 << endl;
  cout << "str3: " << str3 << endl;
  return 0;
}
```

```
Command Prompt                                    _ □ ✕

C:\MyPrograms>c++ string.cpp -o string.exe

C:\MyPrograms>string
str1: Hello from C++
str2: Programming in easy steps
str3: by Mike McGrath
```

Getting string input

The C++ string variables can be assigned the value of other string variables by the = assignment operator. They can also be assigned text from user input using the cin function.

In the example below three string variables are declared, but not initialized. The first two are subsequently assigned text strings from user input. This first string is then copied into the third string variable before being displayed in the generated output.

stringin.cpp

```
#include <string>
#include <iostream>

using namespace std;

int main()
{
    string str1;      //declare three string variables
    string str2;
    string str3;

    cout << "Please enter your first name: ";
    cin >> str1;      //assign first name string to str1

    cout << "Thanks " << str1 << endl;
    cout << "Now please enter your last name: " << str2;
    cin  >> str2;     //assign last name string to str1

    str3 = str1;      //assign first name string to str3
    cout << "Welcome " << str3 << " " << str2 << endl;
    return 0;
}
```

A string variable is automatically resized to accommodate the size of the assigned string.

Command Prompt

```
C:\MyPrograms>c++ stringin.cpp -o stringin.exe

C:\MyPrograms>stringin
Please enter your first name: Mike
Thanks Mike
Now please enter your last name: McGrath
Welcome Mike McGrath

C:\MyPrograms>_
```

A string input problem

The cin function example on the previous page works well to assign user input to a string variable for single characters, or multiple characters forming a single word. The problem is that this technique stops reading the input when it encounters a space.

This means that a string sentence cannot be input this way – as soon as a space is input the string ends.

To demonstrate this problem the program below asks the user to input a string containing spaces. The cin function assigns some of the input to two string variables then displays their contents.

problem.cpp

```cpp
#include <string>
#include <iostream>
using namespace std;

int main()
{
  string str1, str2;

  cout << "Enter any sentence: ";
  cin >> str1;
  cin >> str2;

  cout << "str1: " << str1 << endl;
  cout << "str2: " << str2 << endl;
  cout << "Everything else has been lost\n";
  return 0;
}
```

The first cin function call reads input until it meets a space, then the program moves on to the second cin function call. The solution to this problem is provided on the next page.

```
Command Prompt                                    _ □ ✕

C:\MyPrograms>c++ problem.cpp -o problem.exe

C:\MyPrograms>problem
Enter any sentence: The moon shines bright tonight
str1: The
str2: moon
Everything else has been lost

C:\MyPrograms>_
```

The getline solution

The C++ getline function reads from an input stream until it encounters a \n newline character. It includes spaces so can be used to assign strings with spaces to a string variable.

The standard input from the keyboard is retrieved by the cin function which is added as the first argument in parentheses following the getline name. The second argument is the name of the string variable where the input string should be stored. Optionally a third argument can specify a delimiter character where getline should halt. In this example the \t tab character is set as a delimiter in the second call to the getline function.

getline.cpp

```cpp
#include <string>
#include <iostream>
using namespace std;

int main()
{
    string str1, str2, str3;

    cout << "Enter any sentence: ";
    getline(cin, str1);
    cout << "str1: " << str1 << endl;
    cout << "Enter two words separated by a tab: ";
    getline(cin, str2, '\t');
    getline(cin, str3);
    cout << "str2: " << str2 << endl;
    cout << "str3: " << str3 << endl;
    return 0;
}
```

The example on pages 80/81 demonstrates how the getline function delimiter can be used to format text read from a data file.

```
Command Prompt                                          _ □ ✕

C:\MyPrograms>c++ getline.cpp -o getline.exe

C:\MyPrograms>getline
Enter any sentence: The moon shines bright tonight
str1: The moon shines bright tonight
Enter two words separated by a tab: Big Small
str2: Big
str3: Small
```

Finding the length of a string

The <string> class contains methods that make it easy to work with strings. To use these just add the method after a string variable name and a dot. The size method returns the total number of characters and spaces within a string.

A string can be emptied by assigning an empty string with just two double quotes. It is important not to have any spaces within these quotes or the string will not be completely empty. For instance, a single space within the assigned quotes would give the string a size of 1.

In the example below the value contained in a string variable is displayed, along with its size. The string is then emptied and its new size is displayed.

stringsize.cpp

The <string> class must be included to make its methods available to the

program.

```cpp
#include <string>
#include <iostream>
using namespace std;

int main()
{
  string str = "C++ is fun";

  cout << "Stored string is: " << str << endl;
  cout << "String size is: " << str.size() << endl;
  str = "";   //leave no space between quotes!
  cout << "String cleared" << endl;
  cout << "String size is: " << str.size() << endl;
  return 0;
}
```

```
Command Prompt                                          _ □ ✕

C:\MyPrograms>c++ stringsize.cpp -o stringsize.exe

C:\MyPrograms>stringsize
Stored string is: C++ is fun
String size is: 10
String cleared
String size is: 0

C:\MyPrograms>_
```

Testing for empty strings

Another method of the <string> class is the empty method that returns true (1) or false (0) to report the state of a string variable.

The empty method is useful when requesting input to insist that the user enters at least one character before the program will continue.

This is demonstrated by the program below which queries if a string variable is empty on each iteration of a loop. When the user does enter input it is assigned to the string variable. Now because the string variable is no longer empty the call to the empty method returns false. Consequently the loop ends and the program is able to proceed.

empty.cpp

```cpp
#include <string>
#include <iostream>
using namespace std;

int main()
{
    string name;

    while (name.empty())
    {
        cout << "Please enter your name: ";
        getline(cin, name);
    }
    cout << "Thanks " << name << endl;
    return 0;
}
```

```
C:\ Command Prompt                                    _ □ ✕
C:\MyPrograms>c++ empty.cpp -o empty.exe

C:\MyPrograms>empty
Please enter your name:
Please enter your name:
Please enter your name:
Please enter your name: Mike
Thanks Mike

C:\MyPrograms>_
```

String concatenation

The + addition operator can be used to concatenate two strings into one single long string. Alternatively the append method of the <string> class can be used for concatenation. This method requires either a string of text or the name of a string variable as its argument, stated in the parentheses following its name.

In the following example the append method concatenates a space and a second string onto the end of the initial string. The final call to the cout function demonstrates the same procedure using the + operator to concatenate the strings.

concat.cpp

```cpp
#include <string>
#include <iostream>
using namespace std;

int main()
{
  string firstname, lastname, fullname;

  cout << "Enter your first name: ";
  cin >> firstname;
  cout << "Enter your last name: ";
  cin >> lastname;
  fullname = firstname;
  fullname.append(" ");
  fullname.append(lastname);
  cout << "Thanks " << fullname << endl;
  cout << "Wow! - " << (firstname + " " + lastname);
  return 0;
}
```

The += operator can also be used to append to a string – as shown in the example on the opposite page.

Command Prompt

```
C:\MyPrograms>c++ concat.cpp -o concat.exe

C:\MyPrograms>concat
Enter your first name: Jerry
Enter your last name: Springer
Thanks Jerry Springer
Wow! - Jerry Springer

C:\MyPrograms>_
```

Comparing strings

Two strings can be compared with the == equality operator or the != inequality operator. Alternatively the <string> class provides a compare method that takes the second string variable as its argument. This method compares the ASCII code values of the characters within the strings and returns zero when the strings are identical. When the strings differ it returns -1 when the second string is of lower value or 1 when it is of higher value.

The example below shows how string comparisons can be made with both the == equality operator and the compare method:

compare.cpp

```cpp
#include <string>
#include <iostream>
using namespace std;

int main()
{
  string str1, str2, sum = "Strings are ";

  cout << "Enter a string: ";
  getline(cin, str1);
  cout << "Enter another string: ";
  getline(cin, str2);
  sum += (str1 == str2) ? "identical" : "different";
  if (str1.compare(str2) == 0) sum += ": The same";
  else
  sum += (str1.compare(str2)< 0) ? ": Less" : ": More";
  cout << sum << endl;
  return 0;
}
```

```
C:\ Command Prompt                                    _ □ ✕

C:\MyPrograms>c++ compare.cpp -o compare.exe

C:\MyPrograms>compare
Enter a string: compare me
Enter another string: compare me
Strings are identical: The same value

C:\MyPrograms>compare
Enter a string: COMPARE ME
Enter another string: compare me
Strings are different: Less
```

Copying strings

The contents of a string variable can be copied to another string variable by simple assignation with the = assignment operator. Alternatively the <string> class provides an assign method that can be used for this purpose. This method takes the name of the string variable to be copied as its argument. Additionally this method allows just a part of the original string to be copied by stating the position of the starting character as its second argument and the number of characters to copy as its third argument.

The example below uses both the = assignment operator and the assign method to copy an entire string. Finally it copies 3 characters of the original string, starting at the fourth character.

stringcopy.cpp

```cpp
#include <string>
#include <iostream>
using namespace std;

int main()
{
  string str1 = "I think, therefore I am";
  string str2 = str1;
  string str3;
  str3.assign(str1);

  cout << "str1: " << str1 << endl;
  cout << "str2: " << str2 << endl;
  cout << "str3: " << str3 << endl;

  str3.assign(str1, 4, 3);
  cout << "str3: " << str3 << endl;
  return 0;
}
```

```
C:\ Command Prompt                                        _ □ ✕
C:\MyPrograms>c++ stringcopy.cpp -o stringcopy.exe
C:\MyPrograms>stringcopy
str1: I think, therefore I am
str2: I think, therefore I am
str3: I think, therefore I am
str3: ink
```

Swapping strings

The C++ <string> class provides a swap method that can be used to exchange the contents of two string variables. This method requires the name of the second string variable as its argument.

In the example below the program displays the contents of two string variables then exchanges their contents. The contents of the string variables are displayed again to demonstrate the exchange.

swap.cpp

```cpp
#include <string>
#include <iostream>
using namespace std;

int main()
{
  string str1 = "This is first";
  string str2 = "and this is second";

  cout << "str1: " << str1 << endl;
  cout << "str2: " << str2 << endl;

  str1.swap(str2);
  cout << "str1: " << str1 << endl;
  cout << "str2: " << str2 << endl;
  return 0;
}
```

```
C:\> Command Prompt                                    _ □ ✕
C:\MyPrograms>c++ swap.cpp -o swap.exe

C:\MyPrograms>swap
str1: This is first
str2: and this is second
str1: and this is second
str2: This is first
```

The swap method offers an efficient means of exchanging strings – without this method a temporary string variable would be needed to accomplish the same operation.

Finding substrings

To search an entire string the zero index element would be specified as the starting point.

A string can be searched to see if it contains a specified substring with the find method of the <string> class. This method takes the substring to seek as its first argument and the index number of the character at which to start the search as its second argument. If the substring is successfully found the find method returns the index number of the first occurrence of the substring's first character in the searched string. If the search fails to locate the substring a value named string::npos is returned.

The example below uses the find method to seek a substring and displays an appropriate message upon completion of the search.

find.cpp

```cpp
#include <string>
#include <iostream>
using namespace std;

int main()
{
  string str = "All dressed up with nowhere to go.";
  string sub1 = "somewhere";
  string sub2 = "nowhere";
  unsigned int pos = str.find(sub1, 0);
  cout << "str: " << str << endl;
  if(pos != string::npos)
   cout << sub1 << " found at: " << pos << endl;
  else cout << sub1 << " not found" << endl;
  pos = str.find(sub2, 0);
  if(pos != string::npos)
   cout << sub2 << " found at: " << pos << endl;
  else cout << "Substring not found" << endl;
  return 0;
}
```

```
Command Prompt                                    _ □ ×
C:\MyPrograms>c++ find.cpp -o find.exe

C:\MyPrograms>find
str: All dressed up with nowhere to go.
somewhere not found
nowhere found at: 20
```

String characters start index numbering at zero, not one.

There are several other <string> methods that are related to find. Two of these are find_first_of, and find_first_not_of. Instead of finding the first occurrence of an exact string, as find does, find_first_of finds the first occurrence of any of the characters in a specified string, and find_first_not_of finds the first occurrence of a character that is not any of the characters in the specified string. The find_last_of and find_last_not_of methods work in a similar manner but begin searching at the end of the string then move forwards. Each of these methods are used in the example below.

findof.cpp

```cpp
#include <string>
#include <iostream>
using namespace std;

int main()
{
    string str = "Beauty is in the eye of the beholder";
    int pos = str.find_first_of("or");
    if(pos != string::npos)
        cout << "first: " << pos << endl;
    pos = str.find_first_not_of("or");
    if(pos != string::npos)
        cout << "first not: " << pos << endl;
    pos = str.find_last_of("or");
    if(pos != string::npos)
        cout << "last: " << pos << endl;
    pos = str.find_last_not_of("or");
    if(pos != string::npos)
        cout << "last not: " << pos << endl;
    return 0;
}
```

The first is the "o" in "of", first not is the "B" in "Beauty", last is the "r" in "beholder" and last not is the second "e" in "beholder".

```
C:\MyPrograms>c++ findof.cpp -o findof.exe

C:\MyPrograms>findof
first: 21
first not: 0
last: 35
last not: 34
```

Inserting into a string

A string can be inserted into another string using the insert method of the <string> class. This method requires the index position at which to insert the second string as its first argument, and the string to be inserted as its second argument.

The example below inserts a second string into the original string to create a new longer string:

insert.cpp

```cpp
#include <string>
#include <iostream>
using namespace std;

int main()
{
  string str = "I do like the seaside";
  string sub = "to be beside ";

  cout << "Original string: " << str << endl;
  str.insert(10, sub);
  cout << "New string: " << str << endl;
  return 0;
}
```

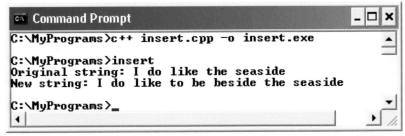

```
C:\MyPrograms>c++ insert.cpp -o insert.exe

C:\MyPrograms>insert
Original string: I do like the seaside
New string: I do like to be beside the seaside

C:\MyPrograms>_
```

This example illustrates again how the string data type is able to dynamically change its size to accommodate whatever length of string is assigned to it.

Erasing and replacing substrings

The opposite method to the insert method, demonstrated opposite, is the erase method that enables specified parts of a string to be removed. Its first argument specifies the index position at which to begin erasing. The second argument specifies the total number of characters to be removed after the starting point.

The replace method neatly combines the erase method and the insert method into one single operation. It specifies the starting point and number of characters to remove, just like the erase method, but has a third argument specifying the string to be inserted after the substring has been removed.

A substring is erased from the original string in the example below then a part of the revised string is replaced:

replace.cpp

```cpp
#include <string>
#include <iostream>
using namespace std;

int main()
{
    string str = "This is an original string";
    cout << str << endl;

    str.erase(9, 10);
    cout << str << endl;

    str.replace(8, 1, "my new");
    cout << str << endl;

    return 0;
}
```

```
C:\MyPrograms>c++ replace.cpp -o replace.exe

C:\MyPrograms>replace
This is an original string
This is a string
This is my new string

C:\MyPrograms>_
```

Getting characters from a string

Individual characters can be retrieved from a string with the <string> class at method. This method requires an index number stating the position of the desired character as its argument.

The final character in a string always has an index number one less than the string size – because the index numbering starts at zero.

In the following example the program retrieves the very first character in the string, a character at a specified position, then the final character in the string:

at.cpp

```cpp
#include <string>
#include <iostream>
using namespace std;

int main()
{
  string str = "I can resist everything but temptation";
  int final = (str.size() - 1);

  cout << "First character: "        << str.at(0) << endl;
  cout << "25th character: "     <<  str.at(25) << endl;
  cout << "String size: "          << str.size() << endl;
  cout << "Last character index: "    << final << endl;
  cout << "Last character: " << str.at(final)  << endl;
  return 0;
}
```

```
C:\ Command Prompt                                    _ □ ✕

C:\MyPrograms>c++ at.cpp -o at.exe

C:\MyPrograms>at
First character: I
25th character: u
String size: 38
Last character index: 37
Last character: n

C:\MyPrograms>_
```

Reading and writing files

This chapter illustrates how C++ programs can create and modify text files. Examples demonstrate how to create new files and show different ways of reading and writing data in files.

Covers

Chapter Six

Writing a file

The ability to read and write files from a program provides a useful method of maintaining data on the computer's hard disk. The format of the data may be specified as human-readable plain text format or machine-readable binary format.

The C++ <fstream> class contains methods for working with files and must be added to the program with an #include directive.

For each file that is to be opened a file object must first be created. This will be an ofstream object for writing output to the file or an ifstream object if reading input from the file. An ofstream object is used just like the cout function that writes to standard output, and the ifstream object is used like the cin function that reads from standard input.

The syntax to create a file object for writing output states the ofstream keyword followed by a space then your chosen name for the file object. Parentheses containing the text file name follow the file object name. For instance, the syntax to create an output file object named "obj" that writes to a file called "myfile.txt" would look like this:

File names should be enclosed within double quotes.

```
ofstream obj("myfile.txt");
```

This argument to the output file object specifying the text file name may optionally contain the full path to the file such as "C:\myfolder\myfile.txt". If no path is specified the program will seek the file within the directory in which the program resides.

Before writing to a file the program should always first check that the file object has been created using an if statement. When this check is successful the program can continue to write output to the specified file. If the file already exists it will, by default, be overwritten without warning. If the file does not exist it will be created.

Upon completion the program should always close the file using the close method of the file object.

The example on the opposite page creates an output file object named "myFile" to write a file named "sky.txt" within the "MyPrograms" folder that contains the C++ example programs.

write.cpp

```cpp
#include <fstream>
#include <string>
#include <iostream>
using namespace std;

int main()
{
  string str = "\n\tI never saw a man who looked";
  str.append("\n\tWith such a wistful eye");
  str.append("\n\tUpon that little tent of blue");
  str.append("\n\tWhich prisoners call the sky\n");

  ofstream myFile("sky.txt");

  if (! myFile)                    // Always test file open
  {
    cout << "Error opening output file" << endl;
    return -1;
  }
  myFile << str << endl;           // Write the file
  myFile.close();                  // Always close the file

  return 0;
}
```

```
C:\MyPrograms>c++ write.cpp -o write.exe

C:\MyPrograms>write
```

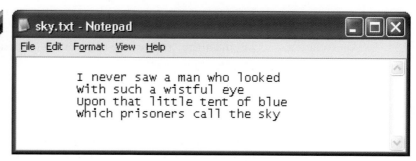

Notice how the newline and tab formatting are preserved in the text file.

sky.txt - Notepad
```
        I never saw a man who looked
        With such a wistful eye
        Upon that little tent of blue
        Which prisoners call the sky
```

Appending to a file

When a file object is created, the parentheses following its given name can optionally contain additional arguments to specify a range of file modes which control the behaviour of that file object. These file modes are listed in the table below together with a description of how the file object can be used:

Mode	Operation
ios::out	open a file to write output
ios::in	open a file to read input
ios::app	open a file to append output at the end of any existing content
ios::trunc	truncate the existing file (default behavior)
ios::ate	open a file without truncating and allow data to be written anywhere in the file
ios::binary	treat the file as binary format rather than text – the data may be stored in a non-text format

Multiple modes may be specified if they are separated by a single pipe character. For instance, the syntax to open a file for binary output could be:

```
ofstream file-object ("file-name", ios::out|ios::binary);
```

The default behavior when no modes are specified considers the file to be a text file that will be truncated when written to.

The most commonly specified mode is ios::app which is used to ensure that existing content will not be overwritten when new output is written to the file. This is used in the example on the opposite page to add the source, date and author's name to the poem in the "sky.txt" text file that was created by the example on the previous page.

append.cpp

```cpp
#include <fstream>
#include <string>
#include <iostream>
using namespace std;

int main()
{
  string str = "\tThe Ballad of Reading Gaol";
  str.append("\n\t\t\tOscar Wilde 1898");

  ofstream myFile("sky.txt", ios::app);

  if (! myFile)                   // Always test file open
  {
    cout << "Error opening output file" << endl;
    return -1;
  }
  myFile << str << endl;          // Write the file
  myFile.close();                 // Always close the file

  return 0;
}
```

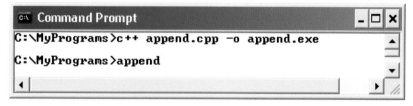

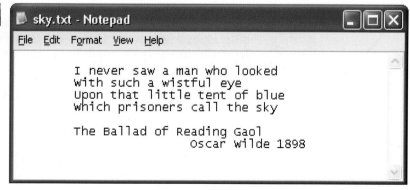

Reading characters

The ifstream file object has a method named get that can be used in a loop to read a file and assign each character in turn into a char variable specified as its argument.

This is used in the example below to read the entire contents of the "sky.txt" text file created earlier in this chapter and display the contents in a console window as standard output:

readchars.cpp

```cpp
#include <fstream>
#include <iostream>
using namespace std;

int main()
{
  char ch;
  ifstream myFile("sky.txt");
  if (! myFile)               // Always test file open
  {
    cout << "Error opening output file" << endl;
    return -1;
  }
  while (! myFile.eof())  // Loop through characters
  {
    myFile.get(ch);
    cout << ch;
  }
  myFile.close();             // Always close the file
  return 0;
}
```

Notice how the ifstream eof method is used to check to see if the "end of file" has been reached.

```
C:\ Command Prompt                              _ □ ✕
C:\MyPrograms>c++ readchars.cpp -o readchars.exe

C:\MyPrograms>readchars

        I never saw a man who looked
        With such a wistful eye
        Upon that little tent of blue
        Which prisoners call the sky

        The Ballad of Reading Gaol
                    Oscar Wilde 1898
```

Reading lines

A more efficient way to read the contents of an ifstream file object is to use the getline method to read the text file line by line. This example specifies the ifstream object as its first argument and a string variable to which each line is assigned as its second argument. Each line is then displayed in a console window as standard output.

readlines.cpp

```cpp
#include <fstream>
#include <string>
#include <iostream>
using namespace std;

int main()
{
  string str;
  ifstream myFile("sky.txt");
  if (! myFile)              // Always test file open
  {
    cout << "Error opening output file" << endl;
    return -1;
  }
  while (! myFile.eof())  // Loop through lines
  {
    getline(myFile, str);
    cout << str << endl;
  }
  myFile.close();           // Always close the file
  return 0;
}
```

The newline characters used for formatting in this example are not copied by the getline method because it stops reading when it encounters a newline. The formatting is maintained by adding an endl to the end of each line.

```
┌─────────────────────────────────────────────────┐
│ ▣  Command Prompt                       _ □ ✕    │
├─────────────────────────────────────────────────┤
│ C:\MyPrograms>c++ readlines.cpp -o readlines.exe │
│                                                  │
│ C:\MyPrograms>readlines                          │
│                                                  │
│          I never saw a man who looked            │
│          With such a wistful eye                 │
│          Upon that little tent of blue           │
│          Which prisoners call the sky            │
│                                                  │
│          The Ballad of Reading Gaol              │
│                      Oscar Wilde 1898            │
│                                                  │
│ ◀                                            ▶   │
└─────────────────────────────────────────────────┘
```

Formatting with getline

The getline method can optionally specify a delimiter at which to stop reading a line. This can be used to separate text read from a tabulated list in a data file. The following example stores each tabulated piece of text in the file on the opposite page as an element of a string array. Each element's content is then displayed in a console window as standard output in a formatted style.

records.cpp

```cpp
#include <fstream>
#include <string>
#include <iostream>
using namespace std;

int main()
{
  string str[20];                  // string array
  int i = 0, j = 0, last;          // counter variables
  ifstream myFile("records.txt");  // input file object
  if (! myFile)                    // always check this
  {
    cout << "Unable to open input file" << endl;
    return -1;
  }

  while (! myFile.eof())           // loop through data
  {
    if ((i + 1) % 4 ==0) getline(myFile, str[i++]);
    else getline(myFile, str[i++], '\t');
  }
  last = i;                        // final element #
  i = 0;
  while (i < last)                 // display records
  {
    cout << "\nRecord Number:\t" << ++j << endl;
    cout << "Forename:\t"   << str[i++] << endl;
    cout << "Surname:\t"    << str[i++] << endl;
    cout << "Department:\t" << str[i++] << endl;
    cout << "Tel.No.:\t"    << str[i++] << endl;
  }
  myFile.close();                  // close the file
  return 0;
}
```

The if-else statements in the first while loop call the getline function to terminate at a tab delimiter – except on every fourth call when it terminates at a newline character.

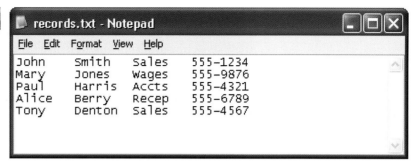

```
records.txt - Notepad
File  Edit  Format  View  Help

John      Smith     Sales     555-1234
Mary      Jones     Wages     555-9876
Paul      Harris    Accts     555-4321
Alice     Berry     Recep     555-6789
Tony      Denton    Sales     555-4567
```

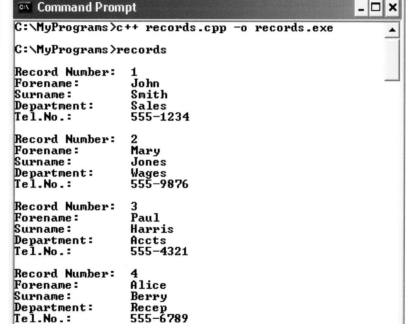

```
Command Prompt

C:\MyPrograms>c++ records.cpp -o records.exe

C:\MyPrograms>records

Record Number:   1
Forename:        John
Surname:         Smith
Department:      Sales
Tel.No.:         555-1234

Record Number:   2
Forename:        Mary
Surname:         Jones
Department:      Wages
Tel.No.:         555-9876

Record Number:   3
Forename:        Paul
Surname:         Harris
Department:      Accts
Tel.No.:         555-4321

Record Number:   4
Forename:        Alice
Surname:         Berry
Department:      Recep
Tel.No.:         555-6789

Record Number:   5
Forename:        Tony
Surname:         Denton
Department:      Sales
Tel.No.:         555-4567

C:\MyPrograms>_
```

Remember to make the string array large enough to hold the maximum number of envisaged strings.

Input/output manipulators

The examples in this chapter have used the default iostream format settings but other settings can be explicitly specified with the C++ input/output manipulators listed in the following table:

The example on page 84 shows how input/output manipulators can be used.

Manipulator	Operation
boolalpha	Outputs bool variables as true or false
noboolalpha (default)	Outputs bool variables a 0 or 1
dec (default)	Displays integers as base 10 (decimal)
hex	Displays integers as base 16 (hexadecimal)
oct	Displays integers as base 8 (octal)
left	Displays text left justified
right	Displays text right justified
internal	Displays numeric sign left justified and the value right justified
noshowbase (default)	Hides a prefix indicating the numeric base
showbase	Displays a prefix indicating the numeric base
noshowpoint (default)	Displays a decimal point only when a number has a fractional part
showpoint	Always displays a decimal point
noshowpos (default)	Hides a + prefix for positive numbers
showpos	Displays a + prefix for positive numbers
skipws	Causes white space (blanks, tabs, newlines) to be skipped by the >> input operator
noskipws	Causes the >> input operator not to skip white space

Manipulator	Operation
fixed (default)	Displays floating point numbers in fixed notation
scientific	Displays floating point numbers in scientific notation
nouppercase (default)	Displays 0x for hexadecimal numbers and e for scientific notation
uppercase	Displays 0X for hexadecimal numbers and E for scientific notation

The manipulators in the above table modify the state of the iostream object. This means that once used on an iostream object they will affect all subsequent input or output done with that object.

The manipulators in the table below, however, are used to format a particular output but do not modify the state of the object:

Manipulator	Operation
setw(w)	Sets the output width to w – needs the <iomanip> class to be included
width(w)	Sets the output width to w using a method of the <iostream> class
setfill(ch)	Fills white space in the output with ch – needs the <iomanip> class to be included
fill(ch)	Fills the white space in the output with ch using a method of the <iostream> class
setprecision(n)	Sets the display of floating point numbers to the precision n – this is a display format that does not affect numeric calculations

setw is an alternative for the width manipulator and setfill is an alternative for the fill manipulator – see the example on the next page.

Using input/output manipulators

The final example in this chapter demonstrates some of the input/output manipulators from the previous page in action:

manip.cpp

```cpp
#include <string>
#include <iomanip>
#include <iostream>
using namespace std;

int main()
{
    string str = "C++ is great";
    double flt = 1.0123456789;
    int num = 15;
    bool flag = 1;
    cout.width(20);
    cout << str << endl;
    cout.width(30);
    cout.fill('x');
    cout << str << endl;
    cout << setw(40) << setfill('.') << str << endl;
    cout << flt << endl;
    cout << setprecision(12) << flt << endl;
    cout << hex << showbase << num << endl;
    cout << oct << showbase << num << endl;
    cout << showpos << dec << num << endl;
    cout << boolalpha << flag << endl;
    return 0;
}
```

```
C:\MyPrograms>c++ manip.cpp -o manip.exe

C:\MyPrograms>manip
        C++ is great
xxxxxxxxxxxxxxxxxxC++ is great
.............................C++ is great
1.01235
1.0123456789
0xf
017
+15
true
```

Using functions

In C++ programming, functions contain pieces of code to be executed whenever the function is called in a program. This chapter demonstrates by example a variety of ways in which functions can be used.

Covers

Chapter Seven

Function basics

Functions are used to enclose a section of code that provides specific functionality to the program. When a function is called from the main program its statements are executed and, optionally, a value can be returned to the main program upon completion. There are three main benefits to using functions:

- They make the program code easier to understand/maintain

- Tried and tested functions can be reused by other programs

- Several programmers can divide the workload in a large project by working on different functions for the program

Declaring functions

Strictly speaking the arguments in a function prototype are known as its "formal parameters".

Each function is declared early in the program code as a prototype comprising a data type for the value it is to return, a function name followed by parentheses which may optionally contain a list of arguments. The syntax for a function declaration looks like this:

```
return-data-type function-name (arguments-list);
```

For instance, the following code declares a function named "writename" that accepts no arguments and returns no value:

```
void writename();
```

Defining functions

Use the void keyword if the function will not return a value to the caller.

The function's definition appears later in the program code and comprises a repeat of the prototype together with the function body. The function body is a pair of braces surrounding the statements that are to be executed whenever this function is called.

It is important to note that the compiler checks the function definition against the function prototype so the return data type must match that in the prototype and any arguments must match in both type and number. Compilation will fail if these differ.

A definition for the function declared above could look like this:

```
void writename()
{
  cout << "Mike McGrath" << endl;
}
```

Variable scope

Variables that are declared in a function can only be used locally within that function and are not accessible globally for use in other functions. This is known as "variable scope".

So in the example program below the variable entitled "name" cannot be used in the main function and the variable named "title" cannot be used in the writename function.

scope.cpp

The aim is to have mostly just function calls in the main function.

```cpp
#include <string>
#include <iostream>
using namespace std;

void writename();   //prototypes (function declarations)
void writetitle();

int main()
{
  writetitle();      //function calls
  writename();
  return 0;
}

void writename()    // function definition
{
  string name = "Mike McGrath";
  cout << name << endl;
}

void writetitle()   // function definition
{
  string title = "C++ Programming in easy steps";
  cout << title << " by ";
}
```

```
Command Prompt                                    _ □ ✕
C:\MyPrograms>c++ scope.cpp -o scope.exe

C:\MyPrograms>scope
C++ Programming in easy steps by Mike McGrath
```

Function arguments

Frequently functions will be passed values as arguments from the caller. These can be of any quantity and data type but they must agree with those specified in the prototype function declaration. Similarly the function can return a value of any data type, as long as it is of the type specified in the function prototype.

The following example demonstrates how to pass values to functions as arguments and how functions return values to the caller. First the main program calls the getnum function to assign user-input values to two int variables. Their values are then passed as arguments to the getmax function which returns the greater of the two values to the caller for display as standard output.

Functions must be declared before they can be used in a program. It is common to place the function prototypes before the main program and the definitions after it.

Next the getftemp function is called to assign a user-input value to an int variable. This value is then passed as an argument to the FtoC function which performs a calculation based on the received value and returns the result to the caller for display.

This simple example illustrates how a C++ program is split into component parts to improve readability and make code maintenance much easier:

args.cpp

```cpp
#include <iostream>              //compiler directives
using namespace std;

int getnum();                    //function prototypes
int getmax(int n1, int n2);
int getftemp();
int FtoC(int faren);

int main()                       //main program
{
  int num1, num2, ftemp;

  num1 = getnum();
  num2 = getnum();
  cout << "Max. number: "<< getmax(num1, num2) << endl;
  ftemp = getftemp();
  cout << ftemp << "F is " << FtoC(ftemp) << "C\n";
  return 0;
}
```

args.cpp
(continued)

```cpp
int getnum()                            //function definitions
{
  int num;

  cout << "Enter a number: ";
  cin >> num;
  return num;
}

int getmax(int n1, int n2)
{
  return (n1 > n2) ? n1 : n2;
}

int getftemp()
{
  int ftemp;

  cout << "Enter Fahrenheit temperature: ";
  cin >> ftemp;
  return ftemp;
}

int FtoC(int ftemp)
{
  float factor = 5.0 / 9.0;
  float freezing = 32.0;
  float celsius;

  celsius = factor * (ftemp - freezing);
  return (int) celsius;
}
```

Variables are only accessible in the function in which they are declared. So the same name of ftemp can be used for the local variables in both the main function and the getftemp function.

```
C:\ Command Prompt                          _ □ ✕
C:\MyPrograms>c++ args.cpp -o args.exe

C:\MyPrograms>args
Enter a number: 567
Enter a number: 345
Max. number: 567
Enter Fahrenheit temperature: 78
78F is 25C
```

Passing arguments by value

When arguments are passed to a function it is important to recognise that it is only the value that is passed, not the variable itself. The function simply receives a copy of the original – this is known as "passing by value".

To illustrate this the program below passes the value of two variables to a function named swap. This function attempts to exchange the values stored in the original variables but fails because it has only received a copy of those variable values.

byvalue.cpp

Functions can change the original variable values through "passing by reference" – see the example on page 121 using "pointers" and the example on page 130 using "references".

```cpp
#include <iostream>
using namespace std;

void swap(int x, int y);

int main()
{
    int x = 4;
    int y = 2;

    cout << "First x is "<< x << ", y is "<< y << endl;
    swap(x, y);
    cout << "Now x is " << x << ", y is " << y << endl;
}

void swap(int x, int y)
{
    int temp;

    temp = y;
    y = x;
    x = temp;
}
```

```
Command Prompt                                    _ □ ✕

C:\MyPrograms>c++ byvalue.cpp -o byvalue.exe

C:\MyPrograms>byvalue
First x is 4, y is 2
Now x is 4, y is 2

C:\MyPrograms>_
```

Setting default argument values

Default values can be assigned to function arguments in the prototype declaration. These will be used unless another value is assigned to that argument in the program. Multiple arguments can be assigned default values but it is important to note that arguments being assigned default values must appear at the end of the argument list after other arguments. The example below assigns a default value to the argument named "margin":

defaults.cpp

Notice that the call to the calcPrice function only requires one argument because the default value is used for the other argument.

```cpp
#include <iomanip>
#include <iostream>
using namespace std;

void calcPrice(float net, float margin = 17.5);

int main()
{
  float net;
  cout << "Enter net cost: ";
  cin >> net;
  calcPrice(net);
  return 0;
}

void calcPrice(float net, float margin)
{
  float profit = (net * margin) / 100;
  cout << showpoint;
  cout << "\nProfit is\t\t\t" << setprecision(3) << profit;
  cout << "\nRetail price inc. profit: ";
  cout << setprecision(4) << (net + profit) << endl;
}
```

The <iomanip> class is added to this example so that the showpoint and setprecision manipulators can format the output to two decimal places.

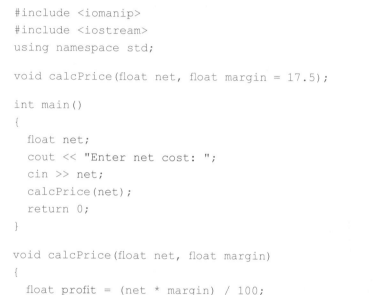

```
C:\MyPrograms>c++ defaults.cpp -o defaults.exe

C:\MyPrograms>defaults
Enter net cost: 10.00

Profit is                    1.75
Retail price inc. profit: 11.75
```

Calling other functions

In the same way that functions can be called from within the main part of a program, functions can call other functions.

This example demonstrating calling other functions gets an integer value from the user then passes it to the showTriple function as an argument. It is passed in turn to the triple function which performs a calculation and returns the result to the caller for output.

callfcn.cpp

```cpp
#include <iostream>
using namespace std;

void showTriple(int n);
int triple(int n);

int main()
{
  int num;
  cout << "Enter a number to triple: ";
  cin >> num;
  showTriple(num);
  return 0;
}

void showTriple(int num)
{
  cout << "3 x "<< num << " = " << triple(num) << endl;
}

int triple(int num)
{
  return (num * 3);
}
```

Note that the names given to prototype arguments need not match those in the function definition, as seen here – only the argument quantity, order and type must match..

```
Command Prompt                                          _ □ ✕

C:\MyPrograms>c++ callfcn.cpp -o callfcn.exe

C:\MyPrograms>callfcn
Enter a number to triple: 8
3 x 8 = 24
```

Recursive functions

A function whose body includes a function call to itself is known as a recursive function. As with a loop, there must be some conditional test within the function by which to exit the recurring execution at some point.

There is some debate in the question of recursion versus iteration but as a recursive function generally runs slower than an equivalent loop it is usually preferable to use a loop. There are, however, some cases, such as algorithms, where the code may be clearer with a recursive function.

The example below demonstrates a simple recursive function:

recur.cpp

```
#include <iostream>
using namespace std;

void recur(int num);

int main()
{
  recur(0);
  return 0;
}

void recur(int num)
{
  cout << "Line " << num << endl;
  num++;
  if (num > 5) return;
  else recur(num);
}
```

A recursive function generally uses more system resources than an equivalent loop.

```
Command Prompt                                    _ □ ✕
C:\MyPrograms>c++ recur.cpp -o recur.exe
C:\MyPrograms>recur
Line 0
Line 1
Line 2
Line 3
Line 4
Line 5
```

Function overloading

Function overloading provides a way to have different functions with the same name. The arguments to each of these functions must differ in number, data type, or both type and number. The compiler will match a function call to the correct function according to the arguments specified in the call. This process is known as function resolution.

It is useful to use function overloading where the functions perform slightly different tasks. The following example overloads three functions that perform essentially the same calculation but to different levels of precision:

overload.cpp

Functions that only differ by their return data type cannot be overloaded – it is the arguments that must differ. Function resolution does not take the return data type into consideration.

```cpp
#include <iomanip>                  //compiler directives
#include <iostream>
using namespace std;

void FtoC(int temp);               //function prototypes
void FtoC(float temp);
void FtoC(double temp);

int main()
{
  int itemp, level;                //variable declarations
  float ftemp;
  double dtemp;

  cout << "CONVERTING FAHRENHEIT TO CELSIUS\n";
  cout << "Select required level of precision\n";
  cout << "Integer (1) - Float (2) - Double (3)\n";
  cin >> level;
  cout << "Enter Fahrenheit temperature: ";

  switch (level)
  {
    case 1 : cin >> itemp; FtoC(itemp); break;
    case 2 : cin >> ftemp; FtoC(ftemp); break;
    case 3 : cin >> dtemp; FtoC(dtemp); break;
    default : cout << "Invalid selection\n";
  }
  return 0;
}
```

overload.cpp
(continued)

```cpp
void FtoC(int itemp)                    //function definitions
{
  int temp = (itemp - 32) * 5 / 9;
  cout << "Integer precision: ";
  cout << itemp << "F is " << temp << "C\n";
}

void FtoC(float ftemp)
{
  float temp = (ftemp - 32) * 5. / 9.;
  cout  << setprecision(8) << "Float precision: ";
  cout << ftemp << "F is " << temp << "C\n";
}

void FtoC(double dtemp)
{
  double temp = (dtemp - 32) * 5. / 9.;
  cout  << setprecision(12) << "Double precision: ";
  cout << dtemp << "F is " << temp << "C\n";
}
```

```
C:\MyPrograms>c++ overload.cpp -o overload.exe

C:\MyPrograms>overload
CONVERTING FAHRENHEIT TO CELSIUS
Select required level of precision
Integer (1) - Float (2) - Double (3)
1
Enter Fahrenheit temperature: 75
Integer precision: 75F is 23C

C:\MyPrograms>overload
CONVERTING FAHRENHEIT TO CELSIUS
Select required level of precision
Integer (1) - Float (2) - Double (3)
2
Enter Fahrenheit temperature: 75
Float precision: 75F is 23.888889C

C:\MyPrograms>overload
CONVERTING FAHRENHEIT TO CELSIUS
Select required level of precision
Integer (1) - Float (2) - Double (3)
3
Enter Fahrenheit temperature: 75
Double precision : 75F is 23.8888888889C
```

Inline functions

Whenever a function is called the program jumps to the location of the function, executes its statements, then returns to a position just after the call to continue onwards. This jumping around slows the program down but can be avoided by declaring a function with the inline keyword in its prototype. Now the compiler will substitute the function's code directly at the point where it is called. For instance, each assignment to the variable named "num" will be compiled as `num = num * num;` in the program below:

inline.cpp

Inline functions are only suitable where the code in the function's body is just one or two lines long. Multiple calls to larger inline functions would make the program much bigger as their entire contents are substituted upon each call to that function.

```cpp
#include <iostream>
using namespace std;

inline int square(int n);

int main()
{
  int num;
  cout << "Enter a number to square: ";
  cin >> num;
  num = square(num);
  cout <<  "Result: " << num << endl;
  num = square(num);
  cout <<  "Result: " << num << endl;
  num = square(num);
  cout <<  "Result: " << num << endl;
  return 0;
}

int square(int n)
{
  return n * n;
}
```

```
Command Prompt                               _ □ ✕
C:\MyPrograms>c++ inline.cpp -o inline.exe

C:\MyPrograms>inline
Enter a number to square: 2
Result: 4
Result: 16
Result: 256
```

Creating classes and objects

This chapter introduces the cornerstones of Object Oriented Programming (OOP). It demonstrates how to create your own classes and objects with unique features and properties.

Covers

Chapter Eight

What is a class?

Fido

A class is a programmer-defined data type that can be used to emulate a real world object. Classes have attributes and actions to simulate those of the real world object. The attributes of a class are known as its "members" and the actions as its "methods".

Any real world object can be defined by its attributes and by its actions. For instance, a dog has attributes such as its age, weight, and color. It also has a set of actions that it can perform such as eat, sleep, and bark. The class mechanism in C++ provides a way to create a virtual dog within a program.

It is important to recognize that a class definition only creates a data type that encapsulates attributes and actions. In order to create an object it is necessary to create an "instance" of that data type. This is achieved in just the same way that instances are created of the regular C++ data types. For example:

```
int x;          //creates an instance of the regular int
                //data type named "x"

Dog Fido        //creates an instance of a programmer-
                //defined Dog data type named "Fido"
```

An object, representing a real world entity, can be manipulated within a program but a class cannot – a class is just a data type. Members of an object can be initialized and assigned values, and its methods can be called by the program. This is the same rule used with regular C++ data types.

Obviously no program class can perfectly emulate a real world object but the aim is to encapsulate all the relevant attributes and abilities.

```
int = 100;   //is incorrect – cannot assign to a class

int x = 100; //is correct – can assign to an instance

Dog.color = "black";      //is incorrect – cannot assign
                          //to a class member

Dog Fido;          //defines an instance of a programmer-
                   //defined Dog class named "Fido"

Fido.color = "black";      //correctly assigns a value
                           //to a color member of the
                           //Dog class instance
```

Defining a class

A class definition begins with the C++ class keyword, followed by a space then a programmer-specified name for the class. The actual members and methods of the class follow next contained within a pair of braces. The class definition must end with a final semicolon after the closing brace.

To allow access to the class members and methods from outside the class the list of members and methods should be preceded by the C++ public keyword, followed by a colon.

For instance, a simplified definition of the Dog class, described on the opposite page, could look like this:

It is conventional to begin class names with an uppercase character.

```
class Dog
{
  public:
    void bark();
    int age;
    int weight;
    string color;
};
```

An instance of the Dog class can now be created in the program by declaring the Dog data type with a programmer-specified name, such as Dog Fido; as shown on the opposite page.

Alternatively an instance of a class can be created by specifying its name between the class definition's closing brace and its final semicolon. Multiple instances can be created this way by specifying a comma-separated list of object names. This definition creates three instances of the Dog class named "Fido", "Rover" and "Pooch":

```
class Dog
{
  public:
    void bark();
    int age;
    int weight;
    string color;
} Fido, Rover, Pooch;
```

Creating an object

An object is an instance of a programmer-specified class that can have data assigned to its members and that has methods which can be called by the program.

The example below defines a class named Dog and creates an object named Fido with three attributes of age, weight and color. These are assigned values which are then displayed in the output.

object.cpp

Remember to include the <string> class for the color member of the Dog class definition.

```cpp
#include <string>
#include <iostream>
using namespace std;

class Dog
{
  public:
    void bark();
    int age;
    int weight;
    string color;
};

int main()
{
  Dog Fido;
  Fido.age = 3;
  Fido.weight = 15;
  Fido.color = "black";
  cout << "Fido is " << Fido.age << " years old\n";
  cout << "Fido weighs " << Fido.weight << " lbs\n";
  cout << "Fido is a " << Fido.color <<  " dog\n";
  return 0;
}
```

```
C:\ Command Prompt                                    _ □ ✕

C:\MyPrograms>c++ object.cpp -o object.exe

C:\MyPrograms>object
Fido is 3 years old
Fido weighs 15 lbs
Fido is a black dog
```

Defining object methods

The definition of a class method outside the class definition must identify the class it refers to. This requires the class name and a double colon :: to precede the method name in the method definition. The :: is a scope resolution operator that indicates that the definition refers to the method in the specified class.

In the example below a definition is given for the bark method of the Dog class, then it is called from the main part of the program:

method.cpp

The scope resolution operator was seen earlier in the examples on pages 68 and 77. There they were used to explicitly identify certain methods of the standard C++ library.

```cpp
#include <string>
#include <iostream>
using namespace std;

class Dog
{
  public:
    void bark();
    int age;
    int weight;
    string color;
};

void Dog::bark()
{
  cout << "WOOF!\n";
}

int main()
{
  Dog Fido;
  Fido.bark();
  return 0;
}
```

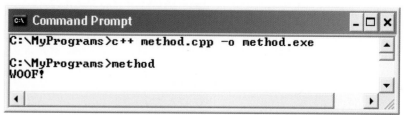

```
C:\MyPrograms>c++ method.cpp -o method.exe

C:\MyPrograms>method
WOOF!
```

Storing data privately

It is more secure to make class members not directly accessible from outside the class to protect their data. This technique is known as "data hiding" and simply means moving the members in the class body to below a private: heading, rather than public:.

In order to assign and retrieve values to those members, special "accessor" methods must be added to the public: part of the class. These will be setter methods (to assign data) and getter methods (to retrieve data). Accessor methods are named after the variable they access but the first letter is made uppercase and the name is prefixed by "set" or "get" respectively.

If the member's name and the argument name do not conflict the "this" pointer is not needed – it is only required for clarity when both are named alike.

Accessor methods must be defined, as usual. Each object has a special pointer named this which refers to the object itself. So object members can be referred to as this -> age, etc.. This can be useful in the accessor method definitions where the argument may often have the same name as the class member. The this pointer can distinguish between the argument and the class member.

The this pointer is used in the following example which adds data hiding to the Dog class described on the previous page:

private.cpp

Notice that all the methods are in the public: section while all the variables are in the private: section. This notion of "public interface, private data" is a key concept when creating classes.

```cpp
#include <string>
#include <iostream>
using namespace std;

class Dog
{
  public:
      void setAge(int age);              //setters
      void setWeight(int weight);
      void setColor(string color);
      int getAge();                      //getters
      int getWeight();
      string getColor();
      void bark();
  private:
      int age;                           //data storage
      int weight;
      string color;
};
```

*private.cpp
(continued)*

```cpp
void Dog::setAge(int age)                    //setter
definitions
{
  this -> age = age;
}

void Dog::setWeight(int weight)
{
  this -> weight = weight;
}

void Dog::setColor(string color)
{
  this -> color = color;
}
```

*The getter
definitions here
have each been
shown on a single
line just to save
page space.*

```cpp
int Dog::getAge() { return age; }    //getter definitions
int Dog::getWeight() { return weight; }
string Dog::getColor() { return color; }

void Dog::bark() { cout << "WOOF!\n"; }

int main()                                   //main program
{
  Dog Fido;
  Fido.setAge(3);
  Fido.setWeight(15);
  Fido.setColor("black");
  cout << "Fido is "<< Fido.getAge() << " years old\n";
  cout << "Fido weighs "<<Fido.getWeight() << " lbs\n";
  cout << "Fido is a " << Fido.getColor() <<  " dog\n";
  return 0;
}
```

```
Command Prompt                                    _ □ ×
C:\MyPrograms>c++ private.cpp -o private.exe

C:\MyPrograms>private
Fido is 3 years old
Fido weighs 15 lbs
Fido is a black dog
```

Constructors and destructors

Class members can be initialized with a special class method called a "constructor". The constructor method requires arguments that will be the initial value of the class members. The method must not state any return value though – not even void. A constructor method must always have the same name as the class name.

Whenever a constructor is declared a matching "destructor" method must also be declared to clean up after the constructor by freeing any memory that may have been allocated to the constructor. A destructor method has the same name as the class name but is preceded by a ~ tilde character. This method takes no arguments and has no return value.

The following example adds a constructor and destructor method to the Dog class seen on the previous page. This allows the Fido object to be created and its members initialized simultaneously.

init.cpp

```
#include <string>
#include <iostream>
using namespace std;

class Dog
{
  public:
    //constructor
    Dog(int initAge, int initWeight, string initColor);

    ~Dog();                              //destructor

    void setAge(int age);                //setters
    void setWeight(int weight);
    void setColor(string color);
    int getAge();                        //getters
    int getWeight();
    string getColor();
    void bark();

  private:
    int age;                             //store data
    int weight;
    string color;
};
```

init.cpp
(continued)

```cpp
//constructor definition
Dog::Dog(int initAge, int initWeight, string initColor)
{
  age = initAge;
  weight = initWeight;
  color = initColor;
}

//destructor definition
Dog::~Dog(){ }

//setter definitions
void Dog::setAge(int yrs) { age = yrs; }
void Dog::setWeight(int lbs) { weight = lbs; }
void Dog::setColor(string clr) { color = clr; }

//getter definitions
int Dog::getAge() { return age; }
int Dog::getWeight() { return weight; }
string Dog::getColor() { return color; }

//class method definition
void Dog::bark() { cout << "WOOF!\n"; }

//main program
int main()
{
  Dog Fido(3, 15, "black");//create & initialize object
  cout << "Fido is " <<Fido.getAge() << " years old\n";
  cout << "Fido weighs "<<Fido.getWeight() << " lbs\n";
  cout << "Fido is a " << Fido.getColor() <<  " dog\n";
  return 0;
}
```

*All method
definitions except
the constructor
have each been
placed on a single
line to save page space.*

```
C:\MyPrograms>c++ init.cpp -o init.exe

C:\MyPrograms>init
Fido is 3 years old
Fido weighs 15 lbs
Fido is a black dog
```

Constant object methods

Methods that never change a class member value should be declared as constant using the const keyword in both the declaration and definition. This should be inserted just after the closing argument parenthesis and helps to prevent errors.

Also methods with just one or two lines of code can be made inline using the inline keyword in just the same way that regular functions can be made inline. A method may include its body code within the class declaration to become automatically inline.

These techniques have been incorporated into the following example which builds upon the Dog class example from the previous page to create two objects as instances of the Dog class:

const.cpp

The definition of a class method is also known as the method "implementation".

```
#include <string>
#include <iostream>
using namespace std;

class Dog
{
  public:
    //constructor
    Dog(int initAge, int initWeight, string initColor);

    ~Dog();                        //destructor

    void setAge(int age);          //setters
    void setWeight(int weight);
    void setColor(string color);

    int getAge() const;            //constant getters
    int getWeight() const;
    string getColor() const;

    //automatically inline constant method
    void bark() const { cout << "WOOF!\n"; };

  private:
    int age;                       //store data
    int weight;
    string color;
};
```

const.cpp
(continued)

```cpp
//constructor definition
Dog::Dog(int initAge, int initWeight, string initColor)
{
  age = initAge;
  weight = initWeight;
  color = initColor;
}

//destructor definition
Dog::~Dog(){ }

//inline setter definitions
inline void Dog::setAge(int yrs) { age = yrs; }
inline void Dog::setWeight(int lbs) { weight = lbs; }
inline void Dog::setColor(string clr) { color = clr; }

//inline constant getter definitions
inline int Dog::getAge() const { return age; }
inline int Dog::getWeight() const { return weight; }
inline string Dog::getColor() const { return color; }

//main program
int main()
{
  Dog Lady(4, 18, "brown");      //create and initialize
  Dog Fido(3, 15, "black");      //two Dog objects

  cout << "Fido is a " << Fido.getColor() << " dog\n";
  cout << "Lady is " << Lady.getAge()<< " years old\n";
  cout << "Lady weighs " <<Lady.getWeight()<< " lbs\n";
  cout << "Lady is a " << Lady.getColor() <<  " dog\n";
  return 0;
}
```

The setter and getter methods in this example have just one line of code each – so they could also usefully be made inline by including their body code within the class declaration in the same way as the bark method.

```
Command Prompt                                   _ □ ✕

C:\MyPrograms>c++ const.cpp -o const.exe

C:\MyPrograms>const
Fido is a black dog
Lady is 4 years old
Lady weighs 18 lbs
Lady is a brown dog
```

Isolating class declarations

Although the previous examples in this chapter have introduced class declarations in the source code file for simplicity, in reality this is not good programming practice. Most programmers place the class declaration in a header file. This normally bears the same name as the main program file but with the file extension ".hpp".

The header file can be used in the main program file by adding an #include compiler directive. This is similar to including a standard C++ class but the header file name, including the file extension, must be enclosed inside double quotes instead of angled brackets.

By isolating class declarations in this way the size of the main source code is greatly reduced and the class becomes modular so it can be used inside any other program simply by adding an appropriate #include directive – another programmer only needs to know the class method names and the number, type and purpose of their arguments to be able to use the class.

The following example is the final rendition of the Dog class developed throughout this chapter. Its main program file, listed below, has an #include directive for the header file shown opposite. All methods in the Dog class are now declared inline.

dog.cpp

```cpp
#include "dog.hpp"          //include class header file

int main()
{
    Dog Lady(4, 18, "brown");     //create & initialize
    Dog Fido(3, 15, "black");     //two Dog objects

    Fido.bark();
    cout << "\tFido is a "<< Fido.getColor() << " dog\n";
    cout << "\tFido is "<< Fido.getAge()<< " years old ";
    cout << "and weighs "<< Fido.getWeight() << "lbs\n";

    Lady.bark();
    cout << "\tLady is a "<< Lady.getColor() << " dog\n";
    cout << "\tLady is "<< Lady.getAge()<< " years old ";
    cout << "and weighs " << Lady.getWeight() << "lbs\n";

    return 0;
}
```

The <iostream> class and <string> class are included in the header file so will also be available to the main program file.

dog.hpp

```cpp
#include <string>
#include <iostream>
using namespace std;

class Dog
{
  public:
    //inline constructor & destructor
    Dog(int initAge, int initWeight, string initColor)
    {
      age = initAge;
      weight = initWeight;
      color = initColor;
    }
    ~Dog() { }

    //inline setters & inline constant getters
    void setAge(int yrs) { age = yrs; }
    void setWeight(int lbs) { weight = lbs; }
    void setColor(string clr) { color = clr; }
    int getAge() const { return age; }
    int getWeight() const{ return weight; }
    string getColor() const{ return color; }

    void bark() const { cout << "WOOF!\n"; }
  private:
    int age;                        //store data
    int weight;
    string color;
};
```

All getter methods can be declared as constant because they will never change the value stored in a class member.

```
Command Prompt                                      _ □ X
C:\MyPrograms>c++ dog.cpp -o dog.exe

C:\MyPrograms>dog
WOOF!
        Fido is a black dog
        Fido is 3 years old and weighs 15lbs
WOOF!
        Lady is a brown dog
        Lady is 4 years old and weighs 18lbs
```

Using classes in other classes

Once a class has been created it can be used within other class declarations by adding an #include compiler directive to the class file. Its methods then become available for use in the next class declaration.

The example program below uses the Point class listed at the top of the opposite page to store the X and Y coordinates of two points of a rectangle. These are retrieved to calculate the area of that rectangle. The Point class is also used to store coordinates in the Rect class declaration at the bottom of the opposite page. The example on page 112 uses the Rect class to display the width, height and area of a rectangle after the coordinates of its top left corner and its bottom right corner have been entered by a user.

area.cpp

```cpp
#include "point.hpp"
#include <iostream>
using namespace std;

int main()
{
  Point topL, btmR;
  int width, height;
  topL.setX(5);
  topL.setY(5);
  btmR.setX(15);
  btmR.setY(15);
  width = btmR.getX() - topL.getX();
  height = btmR.getY() - topL.getY();
  cout << "Rectangle is " << width << " x " << height;
  cout << "\nArea is " << (width * height) << endl;
  return 0;
}
```

```
Command Prompt                                    _ □ X

C:\MyPrograms>c++ area.cpp -o area.exe

C:\MyPrograms>area
Rectangle is 10 x 10
Area is 100
```

point.hpp

```
class Point
{
  public:                    //no constructor - use default
    void setX(int x) { X = x; }         //setters
    void setY(int y) { Y = y; }
    int getX() const { return X; }      //getters
    int getY() const { return Y; }
  private:                              //store data
    int X;
    int Y;
};
```

The Rect class listed below uses the Point class shown above:

rect.hpp

```
#include "point.hpp"

class Rect
{
  public:
    Rect(int topX, int topY, int btmX, int btmY)
    {
      topL.setX(topX);              //Point class methods
      topL.setY(topY);
      btmR.setX(btmX);
      btmR.setY(btmY);
      setWidth(topX, btmX);
      setHeight(topY, btmY);
    }
    ~Rect() {}
    int getWidth() const {return width;}
    int getHeight() const {return height;}
    int Area() const {return getWidth()*getHeight();}
  private:
    Point topL;                     //Point class objects
    Point btmR;
    int width;
    int height;
    void setWidth(int x1, int x2) { width = x2 - x1; }
    void setHeight(int y1, int y2) {height = y2 - y1;}
};
```

Notice how the setWidth and setHeight methods have been made private so they cannot be called manually to set the width and height values from outside the class code.

This example stores the X Y coordinates of two points of a rectangle in a Rect object named "MyBox". Its methods display the rectangle's width, height and area from those coordinates.

rect.cpp

The rect.hpp header file is listed on the previous page together with a point.hpp header file that it includes.

```cpp
#include "rect.hpp"
#include <iostream>
using namespace std;

int main()
{
  int topX, topY, btmX, btmY;
  cout << "\nCALCULATE THE AREA OF A RECTANGLE\n";
  cout << "Please enter X Y coordinates...\n";
  cout << "Top left corner X coordinate:";
  cin >> topX;
  cout << "Top left corner Y coordinate:";
  cin >> topY;
  cout << "Bottom right corner X coordinate:";
  cin >> btmX;
  cout << "Bottom right corner Y coordinate:";
  cin >> btmY;
  Rect MyBox(topX, topY, btmX, btmY);
  cout << "Width is " << MyBox.getWidth() << endl;
  cout << "Height is " << MyBox.getHeight() << endl;
  cout << "Area is " << MyBox.Area() << endl;
  return 0;
}
```

```
Command Prompt                                    _ □ ✕

C:\MyPrograms>c++  rect.cpp -o rect.exe

C:\MyPrograms>rect

CALCULATE THE AREA OF A RECTANGLE
Please enter X Y coordinates...
Top left corner X coordinate:20
Top left corner Y coordinate:25
Bottom right corner X coordinate:35
Bottom right corner Y coordinate:65
Width is 15
Height is 40
Area is 600
```

Pointing to data

In C++ programming, data can be referenced by pointing to the machine address at which it is stored. This chapter introduces pointers and demonstrates how they can be used.

Covers

Chapter Nine

The addressof operator

In order to understand C++ pointers it is helpful to understand how data is stored in your computer. Whenever a variable is declared in a program, space is reserved in the machine's memory to store data assigned to that variable. The reserved space is divided into sequentially numbered memory locations where each location can store one byte of data. The number of bytes reserved depends upon the data type of the variable. The allotted memory is referenced by the unique variable name. Envision the computer's memory as a very long row of slots. Each slot has a unique address, which is expressed in hexadecimal format. It's like a long road of houses – each house contains people and has a unique number, in decimal format. In C++ programs, the houses are slots and the people are the variables.

The & addressof operator can be used to return the memory address of any variable in hexadecimal format. The example below displays the machine address of three variables:

addressof.cpp

```
#include <iostream>
#include <string>
using namespace std;

int main()
{
  int num;
  string str = "Something to say";
  double big;
  cout << "Integer variable starts at "<< &num << endl;
  cout << "String variable  starts at "<< &str << endl;
  cout << "Double variable  starts at "<< &big << endl;
  return 0;
}
```

The locations at which the variables are stored will probably be different on your computer.

```
Command Prompt                                    _ □ ✕
C:\MyPrograms>c++ addressof.cpp -o addressof.exe    ▲

C:\MyPrograms>addressof
Integer variable starts at 0x22ff74
String variable  starts at 0x22ff58
Double variable  starts at 0x22ff40            ▼
◄                                              ► //
```

L-values and R-values

Once memory space has been reserved by a variable declaration a value of the appropriate data type can be stored there using the = assignment operator. For instance, num = 100 takes the value on the right (100) and puts it in the memory referenced by the variable named num.

The value to the left of the = assignment operator is known as the "L-value" and the value to its right is known as the "R-value". The "L" in L-value can be considered to mean "location" and the "R" in R-value can be considered to mean "read".

One important rule in C++ programming is that an R-value cannot appear on the left-hand side of the = assignment operator. On the other hand, an L-value may appear on either side of the = assignment operator. Code that breaks this rule, like the example below, will not compile.

values.cpp

L-values are containers whereas R-values are data.

```cpp
#include <iostream>
using namespace std;

int main()
{
    int num; char letter; float decimal; double big;

    //these are all unacceptable assignments
    //R-values cannot appear to the left of =
    100 = num;
    'A' = letter;
    0.12345 = decimal;
    0.0123456789 = big;
    return 0;
}
```

```
C:\ Command Prompt                                    _ □ ✕
C:\MyPrograms>c++ values.cpp -o values.exe
values.cpp: In function 'int main()':
values.cpp:14: non-lvalue in assignment
values.cpp:15: non-lvalue in assignment
values.cpp:16: non-lvalue in assignment
values.cpp:17: non-lvalue in assignment
```

Introducing pointers

Pointers are a useful part of efficient C++ programming. They are variables that store the memory address of other variables. Pointer variables are declared in just the same way that other variables are declared but the variable name is prefixed by a "*". In this case, it represents the "dereference operator", and merely denotes that the declared variable is a pointer. The pointer's data type must match the data type of the variable it points to.

Declare variables before making other statements – for instance, at the beginning of the main function.

Once declared, a pointer variable can be assigned the address of another variable using the & addressof operator. The variable name should <u>not</u> be prefixed by the * dereference operator in the assignment statement – unless the pointer is initialized immediately in the variable declaration itself.

A pointer variable name, when used alone, references a memory address expressed in hexadecimal.

The example below declares and initializes a pointer named x_ptr. A second pointer, named y_ptr, is declared then initialized later.

point.cpp

The locations at which the variables are stored will be different on your computer.

```cpp
#include <iostream>
using namespace std;

int main()
{
    int x = 8, y = 16;
    int *x_ptr = &x; //declare and initialize a pointer
    int *y_ptr;      //declare another pointer variable
    y_ptr = &y;      //assign an address to this pointer
    cout << "Address of x: " << x_ptr << endl;
    cout << "Address of y: " << y_ptr << endl;
    return 0;
}
```

```
Command Prompt                                  _ □ ✕
C:\MyPrograms>c++ point.cpp -o point.exe

C:\MyPrograms>point
Address of x: 0x22ff8c
Address of y: 0x22ff88
```

Getting values with pointers

When the * dereference operator is used in a variable declaration it merely indicates that the variable being declared is a pointer.

However, when a * dereference operator appears before a pointer variable elsewhere in a program it references the data stored at the address assigned to that pointer.

A pointer variable name, when prefixed by the * dereference operator, references the data stored at the address assigned to that pointer.

This means a program can get the address assigned to a pointer variable just by using its name, or it can get the data stored at that address by prefixing its name with the * dereference operator. The example below builds on the previous example to reveal the data stored at the address assigned to each pointer variable:

deref.cpp

```cpp
#include <iostream>
using namespace std;

int main()
{
    int x = 8, y = 16;
    int *x_ptr = &x;
    int *y_ptr;
    y_ptr = &y;
    cout << "Address of x: " << x_ptr << endl;
    cout << "Value of x: " <<  *x_ptr << endl;
    cout << "Address of y: " << y_ptr << endl;
    cout << "Value of y: " <<  *y_ptr << endl;
    return 0;
}
```

*The * dereference operator is alternatively known as the "indirection" operator.*

```
C:\ Command Prompt                                    _ □ ✕

C:\MyPrograms>c++ deref.cpp -o deref.exe

C:\MyPrograms>deref
Address of x: 0x22ff8c
Value of x: 8
Address of y: 0x22ff88
Value of y: 16
```

Pointer arithmetic

Once a pointer variable has been created with an assigned address it can be reassigned another address or moved using arithmetic.

The ++ increment operator and the -- decrement operator will move the pointer along to the next or previous address for that data type – the larger the data type, the bigger the jump.

Larger jumps can be achieved using the += and -= operators.

In the example below the pointer moves up one place, then again by a further one place, before jumping back down two places:

moveptr.cpp

```
#include <iostream>
using namespace std;

int main()
{
    int nums[] = {1, 2, 3};    //create an integer array

    int *ptr = nums; //assigns the address of 1st element
    cout << "ptr address: " << ptr << " value: " << *ptr;

    ptr++;    //move pointer up one place
    cout << "\nptr address: "<< ptr << " value: "<< *ptr;

    ptr++;    //move pointer up one more place
    cout << "\nptr address: "<< ptr << " value: " <<*ptr;

    ptr -= 2; //move pointer down two places
    cout << "\nptr address: "<< ptr << " value: "<< *ptr;
    cout << endl;
    return 0;
}
```

The *= and /= operators cannot be used to move a pointer.

```
Command Prompt

C:\MyPrograms>c++ moveptr.cpp -o moveptr.exe

C:\MyPrograms>moveptr
ptr address: 0x22ff78 value: 1
ptr address: 0x22ff7c value: 2
ptr address: 0x22ff80 value: 3
ptr address: 0x22ff78 value: 1
```

Pointers and arrays

Pointer arithmetic is especially useful with arrays because the elements in an array occupy consecutive memory places.

Assigning just the name of an array to a pointer automatically assigns it the address of the first element. Incrementing the pointer by one moves the pointer along to the next element.

In the following example a pointer is assigned the name of an array called intArr, which assigns the address of its first element to the pointer. A loop then increments the pointer to each element.

arrayptr.cpp

```
#include <iostream>
using namespace std;

int main()
{
    int intArr[10] = {1, 2, 3, 4, 5, 6, 7, 8, 9, 10};
    int i;
    int *ptr = intArr;        //shorthand for intArr[0]

    for(i = 0; i < 10; i++)
    {
        cout << "Element " << i ;
        cout << " value = " << *ptr << endl;
        ptr++;
    }
    return 0;
}
```

The name of an array acts like a pointer to its first element.

```
Command Prompt                                    _ □ ✕
C:\MyPrograms>c++ arrayptr.cpp -o arrayptr.exe

C:\MyPrograms>arrayptr
Element 0 value = 1
Element 1 value = 2
Element 2 value = 3
Element 3 value = 4
Element 4 value = 5
Element 5 value = 6
Element 6 value = 7
Element 7 value = 8
Element 8 value = 9
Element 9 value = 10
```

Changing variable values

Besides being able to access the value of a variable via a pointer, a pointer can also be used to change the value inside a variable. Use the variable pointer name preceded by the ★ dereference operator to assign a new value of the appropriate data type.

In this example a string array is created along with a pointer to its first element. The dereferenced pointer is assigned a string which changes the value of the arrays first element. The pointer is then moved and assigned another string to change the fourth element.

modvar.cpp

```cpp
#include <string>
#include <iostream>
using namespace std;
void show(string str[]);

int main()
{
  string strArr[4] = {"One", "Two", "Three", "Four"};
  string *ptr = strArr;    //shorthand for strArr[0]
  show(strArr);
  *ptr = "First";          //change 1st element
  ptr += 3;                //move to 4th element
  *ptr = "Last";           //change 4th element
  show(strArr);
  return 0;
}

void show(string str[])
{
  cout << "Strings are: ";
  for(int i = 0; i < 4; i++) cout << str[i] << " ";
  cout << endl;
}
```

```
Command Prompt                                    _ □ ✕

C:\MyPrograms>c++ modvar.cpp -o modvar.exe

C:\MyPrograms>modvar
Strings are: One Two Three Four
Strings are: First Two Three Last
```

Passing pointers to functions

In C++ programs, function arguments pass their data "by value" to a local variable inside the called function. This means that the function is not operating on the original value, but a copy of it. Passing a pointer to the original value instead overcomes this to allow the called function to operate on the original value.

To demonstrate this, the main function in the example below creates a local int variable, named num, together with a pointer to its location. In a call to another function, named triple, the address of the num variable is passed to another pointer. Because the second pointer then also points to the num variable's location it can be used to assign a new value to the original num variable.

passptr.cpp

```
#include <iostream>
using namespace std;
void triple(int *number); //function prototype

int main()
{
  int num = 5;
  int *ptr = &num;            //pointer to num location

  cout <<  "num value is " << num << endl;
  triple(ptr);                //pass num location to function
  cout <<  "num value is now " << num << endl;
  return 0;
}

void triple(int *number)
{
  *number = *number * 3;  //change the value of num
}
```

Notice that the pointer argument must be included in the function prototype.

```
Command Prompt

C:\MyPrograms>c++ passptr.cpp -o passptr.exe

C:\MyPrograms>passptr
num value is 5
num value is now 15
```

Arrays of pointers

A C++ program can contain arrays of pointers in which each element of an array contains the address of another variable.

In the example below five pointers contain the address of individual elements of an int array. A pointer array, named ptrs, assigns the addresses to its five elements. The address of each of its elements, and the value stored there, is displayed by a for loop.

arrintptrs.cpp

```cpp
#include <iostream>
using namespace std;

int main()
{
  int intArr[5] = {1, 2, 3, 4, 5};
  int *ptr0 = &intArr[0]; //address of intArr[0]
  int *ptr1 = &intArr[1]; //address of intArr[1]
  int *ptr2 = &intArr[2]; //address of intArr[2]
  int *ptr3 = &intArr[3]; //address of intArr[3]
  int *ptr4 = &intArr[4]; //address of intArr[4]

  //an array containing all 5 pointers
  int *ptrs[5] = {ptr0, ptr1, ptr2, ptr3, ptr4};

  int i;
  for(i = 0; i < 5; i++)
  {
    cout << "The value stored at " << ptrs[i];
      cout << " is " << *ptrs[i] << endl;
  }
    return 0;
}
```

The value of the counter variable named "i" is substituted for the element index number on each iteration of the loop.

```
 Command Prompt                                      _ □ ✕

C:\MyPrograms>c++ arrintptrs.cpp -o arrintptrs.exe

C:\MyPrograms>arrintptrs
The value stored at 0x22ff68 is 1
The value stored at 0x22ff6c is 2
The value stored at 0x22ff70 is 3
The value stored at 0x22ff74 is 4
The value stored at 0x22ff78 is 5
```

Remember to include a final element for the null character when stating the array size.

A character array that ends with the \0 null character has string status and so can be assigned to a pointer. The name of a string char array acts like a pointer to its first element so the addressof operator is not needed when assigning a string to a pointer.

The program below assigns a single string to a char pointer and three strings to a char array pointer. The address of each element is passed to another function then their contents are displayed.

strptrs.cpp

Notice how the entire string in a char array is referenced by the pointer name alone – without the ★ dereference operator.

To include a space in a string there must actually be a space between the single quotes, like this ' ' – two single quotes together i.e. '' is seen as an empty element and causes a compiler error.

```cpp
#include <iostream>
using namespace std;
void show(char *ptr[]);

int main()
{
  char str[11] = {'C','+','+',' ','f','u','n','\0'};
  char *strPtr = str;      //no addressof operator needed
  char *strArrPtr[3] = {"One", "Two", "Three"};
  cout << strPtr << endl;
  show(strArrPtr);
  return 0;
}

void show(char *ptr[])
{
  int i = 0;
  while(i < 3)
  {
    cout << ptr[i] << "\t";
    i++;
  }
}
```

```
Command Prompt                                    _ □ ✕
C:\MyPrograms>c++ strptrs.cpp -o strptrs.exe

C:\MyPrograms>strptrs
C++ fun
One        Two        Three
```

Pointing to functions

Pointers can point to functions, although this ability is used less often than for pointers that point to data values.

A pointer to a function is like a pointer to data but must always be enclosed in plain brackets when using the * dereference operator to avoid a compiler error. These will be followed by plain brackets containing any arguments to be passed to the function when using the * dereference operator.

This example contains a pointer to a function named add which takes two arguments and returns an int data type. The pointer declaration must match the number of arguments and return type of the function it points to. The function is called, via the pointer, to return the sum total of two integers passed to it as arguments.

fcnptr.cpp

Working with pointers takes a little practice – a pointer contains an address, and dereferencing a pointer will access the data value stored at that address. However, an entire string value in a char pointer can be referenced using just the pointer name alone.

```cpp
#include <iostream>
using namespace std;
int add(int x, int y);              //function prototype

int main()
{
   int (*ptr)(int x, int y);        //pointer declaration
   int x = 8, y = 16;
   ptr = add;                       //point to add function
   cout << x << " plus " << y << " equals ";
   //now call the add function via the pointer
   cout << (*ptr)(x, y) << endl;
   return 0;
}

int add(int x, int y)
{
   return x + y;
}
```

```
C:\ Command Prompt                                  _ □ ✕

C:\MyPrograms>c++ fcnptr.cpp -o fcnptr.exe

C:\MyPrograms>fcnptr
8 plus 16 equals 24
```

Referencing data

This chapter illustrates how references can be created within a C++ program. Examples demonstrate how references may be used with data and objects and to improve program flexibility.

Covers

Chapter Ten

What is a reference?

A reference is an alias for an object or variable within a C++ program. A reference must be initialized within its declaration by assigning it the name of the target to which it refers. From then on the reference acts as an alternative name for the target – anything that happens to the reference is really done to the target.

Don't confuse the & reference operator with the & addressof operator – the compiler recognizes each according to the context in which it appears.

A reference declaration states the data type of the target, followed by a space and the & reference operator, then the chosen name of the reference. It is common practice to name the reference with the name of the target using an uppercase first letter and prefixed by an "r", as seen in this declaration:

```
int &rSome Int = someInt;
```

The example below creates a reference using the syntax above and illustrates how the value stored in the variable can be accessed at any time via its reference:

ref.cpp

```
#include <iostream>
using namespace std;

int main()
{
  int someInt;
  int &rSomeInt = someInt;        //reference declaration

  someInt = 500;

  cout << "Variable value is " << someInt << endl;
  cout << "Via reference too it's "<< rSomeInt << endl;
  return 0;
}
```

```
Command Prompt                                    _ □ ✕
C:\MyPrograms>c++ ref.cpp -o ref.exe

C:\MyPrograms>ref
Variable value is 500
Via reference too it's 500
```

Referencing variables

References are such true aliases to their target that when the addressof operator is used on a reference it returns the address of its target. There is no way to discover the location of a reference itself – but there is no reason why its location would be of any use.

Once a reference has been created it will always refer to its initial target and cannot be reassigned to refer to another target. Attempting to do so simply assigns the value of the intended new target to the original target. The example below demonstrates how the addressof operator returns the location of its target, and illustrates the effect of trying to reassign a reference:

refvar.cpp

References always refer to the target to which they have been initialized – a reference cannot be reassigned.

```cpp
#include <string>
#include <iostream>
using namespace std;

int main()
{
  string str = "Original text";
  string newStr = "Updated text";
  string &rStr = str;       //reference declaration
  cout << "str value: " << str;
  cout << " - location: " << &str << endl;
  cout << "rStr reference location: " << &rStr << endl;
  cout << "newStr location: " << &newStr << endl;
  rStr = newStr;            //try to reassign reference
  cout << "str value: " << str;
  cout << "  - location: " << &str << endl;
  cout << "rStr reference location : "<< &rStr << endl;
  return 0;
}
```

```
Command Prompt                                    _ □ ✕

C:\MyPrograms>c++ refvar.cpp -o refvar.exe

C:\MyPrograms>refvar
str value: Original text - location: 0x22ff68
rStr reference location: 0x22ff68
newStr location: 0x22ff58
str value: Updated text  - location: 0x22ff68
rStr reference location : 0x22ff68
```

Referencing objects

In addition to referencing variable data, references can be created for any object, including user-defined objects. It is important to remember, however, that a reference cannot refer directly to a class, but only instances of a class. This rule follows the same principle that only named variables can be assigned to a reference, not a data type. For example:

```
int &rSomeInt = int;           //is not allowed   ✘

int &rSomeInt = myInt;         //is allowed        ✓
```

Similarly when creating references to an object...

```
Dog &rFido = Dog               //is not allowed   ✘

Dog &rFido = Fido;             //is allowed        ✓
```

References to objects can be used in just the same way as the object itself. Its member data and methods are accessed by appending the dot operator and the member name to the reference name in the usual way.

The example below creates a reference to an instance of the Dog class that is listed on the opposite page. It demonstrates how the class methods can be used with a reference to an object.

refobj.cpp

```cpp
#include "dog.hpp"

int main()
{
  //create and initialize an instance of the Dog class
  Dog Fido(3, 15, "black");

  //create a reference to the instance object
  Dog &rFido = Fido;

  rFido.setAge(4); //call a setter method

  //call getter methods
  cout << "Fido is a " << rFido.getColor() << " dog\n";
  cout << "Fido is " <<rFido.getAge() <<" years old\n";
  cout << "Fido weighs "<< rFido.getWeight()<< "lbs\n";
  return 0;
}
```

dog.hpp

For more on this class, and isolating classes in header files, please refer back to Chapter 8.

```cpp
#include <string>
#include <iostream>
using namespace std;

class Dog
{
  public:
    //constructor and destructor methods
    Dog(int initAge, int initWeight, string initColor)
    {
      age = initAge;
      weight = initWeight;
      color = initColor;
    }
    ~Dog() { }

    //setter and getter methods
    void setAge(int yrs) { age = yrs; }
    void setWeight(int kgs) { weight = kgs; }
    void setColor(string clr) { color = clr; }
    int getAge() const { return age; }
    int getWeight() const{ return weight; }
    string getColor() const{ return color; }
    void bark() const { cout << "WOOF!\n"; }

  //store data
  private:
    int age;
    int weight;
    string color;
};
```

```
Command Prompt                                    _ □ ×
C:\MyPrograms>c++ refobj.cpp -o refobj.exe

C:\MyPrograms>refobj
Fido is a black dog
Fido is 4 years old
Fido weighs 15lbs
```

Passing arguments by reference

In C++ programs function arguments pass their data "by value" to a local variable inside the called function. This means that the function is not operating on the original value, but a copy of it. Passing a reference to the original value instead overcomes this to allow the called function to operate on the original value.

To demonstrate this, the main function in the example below creates a local int variable, named score, together with a reference to it named rScore. In a call to another function, named cube, the rScore reference is passed as an argument. Because the rScore reference refers to the original score variable it can be used to assign it a new value from within the cube function.

passref.cpp

Notice that the reference argument must be included in the function prototype.

```cpp
#include <iostream>
using namespace std;

void cube(int &ref);        //function prototype

int main()
{
  int score = 3;
  int &rScore = score;    //reference to score

  cout <<  "score is " << score << endl;
  cube(rScore);             //pass reference to function
  cout <<  "score is now " << score << endl;
  return 0;
}

void cube(int &ref)
{
  ref = ref * ref * ref; //change the value of score
}
```

```
In Command Prompt                                    _ □ ✕
C:\MyPrograms>c++ passref.cpp -o passref.exe

C:\MyPrograms>passref
score is 3
score is now 27
```

Functions can only return a single item of one specified data type but this limitation can be overcome with references and pointers. Passing by reference permits the function to effectively bypass the single return restriction and allows any number of data type values to be changed. This example changes several different values:

multiref.cpp

```cpp
#include <string>
#include <iostream>
using namespace std;

void change(string &sRef, int &iRef, char &cRef);

int main()
{
  string str = "Start: ";
  string &rStr = str;
  int num = 100;
  int &rNum = num;
  char ltr = 'A';
  char &rLtr = ltr;

  cout << str << num << ltr << endl;
  change(rStr, rNum, rLtr);
  cout << str << num << ltr << endl;
  return 0;
}

void change(string &sRef, int &iRef, char &cRef)
{
    sRef = "Finish: ";
    iRef = 555;
    cRef = 'Z';
}
```

The examples on these pages could alternatively have employed pointers to achieve the same results – see overleaf for a comparison of pointers and references.

```
C:\MyPrograms>c++ multiref.cpp -o multiref.exe

C:\MyPrograms>multiref
Start: 100A
Finish: 555Z
```

To reference or to point?

Pointers and references can both be used to refer to variable values and it is technically more efficient to pass these by reference than by value. C++ programmers much prefer using references rather than pointers because they are easier to use and also they are easier to understand.

References must, however, obey certain rules which can make the use of pointers necessary. In particular it should be noted that a reference cannot contain a null value. A program that does so may compile but will not perform correctly.

The following table compares references with pointers:

Rule	References	Pointers
Can be declared without initialization	No	Yes
Can be reassigned	No	Yes
Can contain a null value	No	Yes
Easy to use	Yes	No
Most efficient	Yes	No

As a general rule the choice between using references or pointers can be determined by following these guidelines:

- If you don't want to initialize in the declaration, use a pointer

OR

- If you want to be able to reassign another value, use a pointer

OR

- If there is any possibility that a NULL value may be assigned, use a pointer

OTHERWISE

- Always use a reference.

A program may use both references and pointers – for instance, it is perfectly legal to specify both references and pointers as arguments to a function call.

Inheriting features

This chapter explores deeper into C++ user-defined classes and illustrates how class instances inherit features from the base class from which they are derived. Examples demonstrate how programs can best use the principle of inheritance.

Covers

Chapter Eleven

What is inheritance?

To understand the principle of inheritance it is necessary to recognize that all things are derived from some basic group. For instance, a domestic cat is a type of mammal which is, in turn, a type of animal.

Mammals all have certain common properties, such as breathing air and sleeping. These are not necessarily common properties of all animals, however, but are specialized properties of mammals. A wildcat, such as a tiger, shares these common properties with a domestic cat but has its own specialized properties such as hunting food whereas a domestic cat will rely on its owner for meals.

These hierarchical relationships can be seen everywhere – a Ferrari is a type of car which is, in turn, a type of vehicle – a lettuce is a type of vegetable which is, in turn, a type of plant – and so on.

Each level of the hierarchy automatically inherits the properties of the levels above. For instance, because mammals by definition breath air and sleep then all mammals must breath air and sleep.

C++ can use classes to represent this hierarchical relationship by deriving a class from a higher level class. The class from which a derived class inherits properties is known as its "base" class.

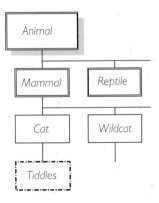

It would be appropriate to derive a Cat class from a higher level Mammal class. Methods and data common to all mammals could be specified in the Mammal class whereas methods and data special only to cats could be specified in the Cat class. For instance, all mammals have an age and a weight so this data could be declared in the base Mammal class but only cats purr so a purr method could be specified in the derived Cat class.

A class declaration can optionally state the class from which it is derived by adding a colon, derivation type and the base class name after its own class name. So the syntax to declare a Cat class derived from a Mammal class looks like this:

```
class Cat : public Mammal
```

The base class must be declared before the derived class to avoid a compiler error. In this case, the Mammal class must be declared before the Cat class declaration.

Protecting class data

Members of a base class which are private are not available to a derived class. This could be remedied by declaring them as public members but it is not really desirable to have them accessible to all classes. A better solution is to declare them as protected members – which makes them accessible only to derived classes.

Accessor specifiers can be public, private or protected.

The code below creates the Mammal class described on the previous page and declares its age and weight members as protected. It has accessor methods for these variables and declares a speak method to output a default "sound".

All of the methods declared in the Mammal class will be accessible from any class derived from it, such as a Cat class. This applies even if there are intermediate classes (DomesticAnimals for instance) layered between the base class and the derived class as long as these classes all use public inheritance.

mammal.hpp

C++ programs cannot accurately duplicate the complexity of all real world relationships but the programmer must decide where to begin the hierarchy – in this example, the higher level of Animal has deliberately been ignored although this could have been used as the base class.

```cpp
#include <iostream>
using namespace std;

class Mammal
{
  public:

    //empty constructor & destructor
    Mammal() { };
    ~Mammal() { };

    //inline setters & getter methods
    void setAge(int yrs) { age = yrs; }
    void setWeight(int lbs) { weight = lbs; }
    int getAge() const { return age; }
    int getWeight() const{ return weight; }

    //inline constant method
    void speak() const { cout << "MAMMAL SOUND!\n"; }

  protected:

    //variables to store data
    int age;
    int weight;
};
```

Creating a derived class

The example below begins with an #include directive to make the Mammal class (listed on the previous page) accessible in order to declare a class named Cat that is derived from the Mammal class:

cat.hpp

```cpp
#include "mammal.hpp"
#include <string>


class Cat : public Mammal
{
  public:

    //constructor & destructor
    Cat(string initName)
    {
      name = initName;
    };
    ~Cat() { };

    //inline getter method
    string getName() const { return name; }

    //inline constant method
    void purr() const { cout << "PRRR!\n"; }

  protected:

    //variables to store data
    string name;
};
```

The Cat class constructor requires a single string argument that is stored in a protected string member variable. An accessor getter method is declared to retrieve this variable's value but as this is permanently set when a Cat object is created a setter method is not needed. A public member method named purr is also declared in the Cat class that will output a "sound" special to cats.

It is now a simple matter to #include the Cat class (incorporating the Mammal class) into a main program to allow the creation of Cat objects that will inherit all the properties of both the derived Cat class and its base Mammal class.

The example below begins with an #include directive to make all members of the derived Cat class, and its base Mammal class, accessible to the program.

An instance of the Cat class creates an object named MyCat and its argument specifies a value to be stored in the name variable. Setter accessor methods specify values to be stored in the age and weight variables. The stored variable values are retrieved for output and the purr and speak member methods are called.

mycat.cpp

Tiddles

```cpp
#include "cat.hpp"

int main()
{
  Cat MyCat("Tiddles");

  MyCat.setAge(3);
  MyCat.setWeight(2);
  MyCat.purr();
  cout << "My cat\'s name is " << MyCat.getName();
  cout << endl;
  cout << MyCat.getName() << " is ";
  cout << MyCat.getAge() << " years old\n";
  cout << MyCat.getName() << " weighs ";
  cout << MyCat.getWeight() << " lbs\n";
  MyCat.speak();
  return 0;
}
```

```
Command Prompt                                        _ □ X
C:\MyPrograms>c++ mycat.cpp -o mycat.exe

C:\MyPrograms>mycat
PRRR!
My cat's name is Tiddles
Tiddles is 3 years old
Tiddles weighs 2 lbs
MAMMAL SOUND!

C:\MyPrograms>_
```

Overloading class constructors

Multiple "overloaded" constructor methods can be declared to allow different numbers of arguments, or different types of arguments, to be specified when an object is created.

The following example modifies that on the preceding pages to provide overloaded constructors in the Cat class. Additionally simple cout statements have been added to every constructor and destructor method to demonstrate when they are called.

cat2.hpp

The header file named mammal2.hpp (included in this example) is the same as the mammal.hpp header file listed on page 135 – however, it has simple cout statements added to the constructor and destructor methods.

```cpp
#include "mammal2.hpp"
#include <string>
class Cat : public Mammal
{
    public:
        Cat(string initName)          //constructors
          {
            name = initName;
            cout << "Cat constructor - setting name\n";
          };
        Cat(string initName, int initAge)
          {
            name = initName;
            age = initAge;
            cout << "Cat constructor ";
            cout << "- setting name & age\n";
          };
        Cat(string initName, int initAge, int initWeight)
          {
            name = initName;
            age = initAge;
            weight = initWeight;
            cout << "Cat constructor ";
            cout << "- setting name, age & weight\n";
          };

        ~Cat() { cout<< "Cat destructor:" << name << "\n"; }
        string getName() const { return name; }
        void purr() const { cout << "PRRR!\n"; }
    protected:
        string name;
};
```

mycat2.cpp

```cpp
#include "cat2.hpp"

int main()
{
  Cat MyCat("Tiddles", 2, 3);
  cout << "My cat\'s name is " << MyCat.getName();
  cout << "\nHe\'s " << MyCat.getAge() << " years old";
  cout <<" and weighs "<< MyCat.getWeight()<< " lbs\n";

  Cat HisCat("Felix", 5);
  cout << "My cat\'s name is " << HisCat.getName();
  cout << " and he\'s " << HisCat.getAge();
  cout << " years old\n";

  Cat HerCat("Whiskers");
  cout << "My cat\'s name is " << HerCat.getName();
  cout << endl;
  HerCat.purr();
  cout << endl;
  return 0;
}
```

When a Cat object is created the appropriate constructor is called to set variables with the specified call arguments and display relevant output.

```
C:\ Command Prompt                                    _ □ ✕

C:\MyPrograms>c++ mycat2.cpp -o mycat2.exe

C:\MyPrograms>mycat2

Mammal constructor
Cat constructor - setting name, age & weight
My cat's name is Tiddles
He's 2 years old and weighs 3 lbs

Mammal constructor
Cat constructor - setting name & age
My cat's name is Felix and he's 5 years old

Mammal constructor
Cat constructor - setting name
My cat's name is Whiskers
PRRR!

Cat destructor: Whiskers
Mammal destructor
Cat destructor: Felix
Mammal destructor
Cat destructor: Tiddles
Mammal destructor
```

Notice that the destructor methods are called to destroy the objects in the reverse order to which they were created.

Overriding base class methods

A derived class can declare a method to override a method in its base class. The method declaration in the derived class must exactly match the method in the base class in order to override it. That means it must have the same return type, name, arguments and the const keyword if it has been used.

Overriding methods in a derived class can hide overloaded methods in its base class.

Care must be taken when overriding base class methods to avoid unintentionally hiding overloaded methods – a single overriding method in a derived class will hide all overloaded methods of that name in the base class!

For instance, the base Mammal class, listed below, contains two overloaded methods named walk. These require no argument and one argument respectively. The derived Cat class, listed on the opposite page, creates an overriding method named walk, with no arguments. This hides <u>both</u> walk methods in the base class.

mammal3.hpp

```cpp
#include <iostream>
using namespace std;

class Mammal
{
  public:

  //use default constructor & destructor

  //inline constant method
  void speak() const { cout << "MAMMAL SOUND!\n"; }

  //overloaded walk methods
  void walk()  const { cout << "Walks 1 foot\n"; }
  void walk(int m)
  {
    cout << "Walks " << m << " feet\n";
  }
};
```

Additionally the Cat class contains a method named speak that will override the method of the same name in the Mammal base class whenever it is called from the main program.

cat3.hpp

```cpp
#include "mammal3.hpp"
#include <string>
class Cat : public Mammal
{
  public:

    //constructor & destructor methods
    Cat(string initName) { name = initName; };
    ~Cat() { };

    string getName() const { return name; }
    void purr() const { cout << "PRRR!\n"; }

    //overriding methods
    void walk() const { cout << "Walks away\n"; }
    void speak() const { cout << "MEOW!\n"; }

  protected:
    string name;
};
```

Remember to include the const keyword to exactly match the base class walk method.

mycat3.cpp

```cpp
#include "cat3.hpp"

int main()
{
  Cat MyCat("Tiddles");
  cout << "My cat\'s name is " << MyCat.getName();
  cout << endl;
  MyCat.speak();    //call overriding speak method
  MyCat.walk();     //call overriding walk method
  //MyCat.walk(3); - would cause a compiler error!

  return 0;
}
```

The example on the next page shows you how to call overridden base class methods directly.

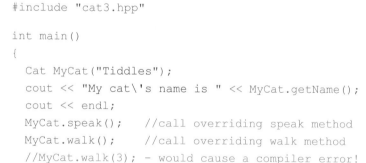

```
Command Prompt                                    _ □ ✕

C:\MyPrograms>c++ mycat3.cpp -o mycat3.exe

C:\MyPrograms>mycat3
My cat's name is Tiddles
MEOW!
Walks away
```

Calling overridden base methods

Any base class method can be called by explicitly stating its class and name, separated by the :: double-colon scope operator. This is useful to call base class methods that have been overridden by derived class methods.

It is important to get the syntax order correct by ensuring that the base class name and the scope operator immediately precedes the object name. The syntax looks like this:

```
object-name.base-class-name::method-name();
```

The following example demonstrates how to explicitly call the two overridden base walk class methods in the previous example. It uses the same mammal3.hpp and cat3.hpp header files listed on pages 140–141.

mycat4.cpp

```cpp
#include "cat3.hpp"

int main()
{
  Cat MyCat("Tiddles");
  cout << "My cat\'s name is " << MyCat.getName();
  cout << endl;
  MyCat.speak();
  MyCat.walk();

  MyCat.Mammal::walk();  //call overridden method
  MyCat.Mammal::walk(3); //call overridden method

  return 0;
}
```

```
Command Prompt                                    _ □ ✕

C:\MyPrograms>c++ mycat4.cpp -o mycat4.exe

C:\MyPrograms>mycat4
My cat's name is Tiddles
MEOW!
Walks away
Walks 1 foot
Walks 3 feet
```

Harnessing polymorphism

This chapter demonstrates advanced use of classes and virtual functions to create polymorphic capability. Examples illustrate the advantage of making a base class into an Abstract Data Type (ADT) and reveal how complex hierarchies can be formed by deriving ADTs from other ADTs.

Covers

Chapter Twelve

Virtual base methods

The three cornerstones of Object-Oriented Programming are encapsulation, inheritance and polymorphism. Previous examples have demonstrated how data can be encapsulated within a C++ class and how derived classes inherit the properties of their base class. This chapter introduces the final cornerstone principle of polymorphism.

The term "polymorphism" (from Greek meaning "many forms") describes the ability to assign a different meaning, or purpose, to an entity according to its context.

Pigeon

In C++, overloaded operators can be described as polymorphic. For instance, the ★ character can represent either the multiply operator or the dereference operator according to its context. More importantly, C++ has the ability to bind specific derived class objects to base class pointers to create polymorphic methods.

The key to creating a polymorphic method is to first declare a "virtual" base class method – this is just a regular declaration preceded by the virtual keyword. The declaration of a virtual method indicates that the class will be used as a base class from which another class will be derived. This derived class will contain a method to override the virtual base method.

A pointer to the base class can be assigned an object of the derived class. This pointer can be used to access regular methods of the base class and overriding methods of the derived class. For instance, this statement assigns a new Pigeon class object (derived from a Bird base class) to a pointer to the Bird base class:

The pointer is assigned the address of the new Pigeon object – this is legal because a Pigeon is a Bird. The compiler only knows that pBird is a Bird so looks in the base class for any method calls. If a base method is declared as virtual the compiler will look in any derived classes instead, to call the overriding method.

```
Bird *pBird = new Pigeon;
```

Almost magically, this pointer can be used to access regular methods of the Bird base class and overriding methods of the derived Pigeon class.

The example listed on the opposite page demonstrates this technique in action. Two methods named Walk and Talk are declared in the base class – but only Talk is a virtual method. When the Talk method is called it executes the overriding method in the derived class, rather than the default statement in the base class, unless the base method is called explicitly.

virtual.cpp

```cpp
#include <iostream>
using namespace std;

class Bird
{
  public:
    //use default constructor & destructor

    //declare a regular method
    void Walk() const { cout << "Walks a few steps\n";
}

    //declare a virtual method
    virtual void Talk() const { cout << "WARBLE!\n"; }
};

class Pigeon : public Bird
{
  public:
    //use default constructor & destructor

    //declare an overriding method
    void Talk() const { cout << "COO! COO!\n"; }
};

int main()
{
  Bird *pPigeon = new Pigeon;    //declare pointer

  pPigeon -> Walk();               //regular method call
  pPigeon -> Talk();               //virtual method call
  pPigeon -> Bird::Talk(); //explicit base method call
  return 0;
}
```

The -> class pointer operator is used to call methods of the base class that the pointer points to – or its overriding method in a derived class.

```
C:\ Command Prompt

C:\MyPrograms>c++ virtual.cpp -o virtual.exe

C:\MyPrograms>virtual
Walks a few steps
COO! COO!
WARBLE!
```

Multiple virtual method calls

This example largely builds upon the previous example by demonstrating the advantage of polymorphism with multiple derived class objects – calls to methods of the same name are directed to the appropriate overriding method:

bird.hpp

```cpp
#include <iostream>
using namespace std;

class Bird
{
  public:
    //use default constructor & destructor
    //declare virtual methods
    virtual void Talk() const
      { cout << "A bird talks...\n"; }
    virtual void Fly()  const
      { cout << "A bird flies...\n"; }
};
```

birds.hpp

```cpp
#include "bird.hpp"

class Pigeon : public Bird
{
  public:
    //use default constructor & destructor
    //declare overriding methods
    virtual void Talk() const { cout << "COO! COO!\n";}
    virtual void Fly()  const
      { cout << "Pigeon flies away...\n"; }
};

class Chicken : public Bird
{
  public:
    //use default constructor & destructor
    //declare overriding methods
    virtual void Talk() const
      { cout << "CLUCK! CLUCK!\n"; }
    virtual void Fly() const
      { cout << "I\'m just a chicken - I can\'t fly!\n";}
};
```

The overriding methods can optionally be declared without using the virtual keyword – but it's a good idea to keep it to remind you that this is an overriding method.

birds.cpp

```cpp
#include "birds.hpp"

int main()
{
  Bird *pPigeon = new Pigeon;      //declare pointers
  Bird *pChicken = new Chicken;

  pPigeon -> Talk();               //virtual method calls
  pPigeon -> Fly();
  pChicken -> Talk();
  pChicken -> Fly();
  pPigeon ->  Bird::Talk();        //explicit base calls
  pChicken -> Bird::Fly();
  return 0;
}
```

```
Command Prompt                                    _ ☐ ✕
C:\MyPrograms>c++ birds.cpp -o birds.exe

C:\MyPrograms>birds
COO! COO!
Pigeon flies away...
CLUCK! CLUCK!
I'm just a chicken - I can't fly!
A bird talks...
A bird flies...
```

In this case the Bird base class contains no regular methods at all but notice that it does contain statements that can be executed if its methods are explicitly called.

Calls to these methods using the derived class object pointers execute the overriding method statements in the appropriate class to which the pointer refers. This acts as expected as illustrated by the previous example.

However, the danger of calling base methods explicitly is amply demonstrated in this example. The explicit call to the Fly method using the pChicken pointer executes the base method's default statement – this would seem to imply that chickens can fly! The example on the next page shows how this can be avoided.

Capability classes

Classes whose sole purpose is to allow other classes to be derived from them are known as "capability classes" – they provide capabilities to their derived classes.

Capability classes generally contain no data but merely specify a number of virtual methods that can be overridden in their derived classes.

The following example builds on the previous example to demonstrate how the Bird class can be better written as a capability class. Its methods no longer contain default output statements but return a -1 (error) value if they are called explicitly.

It is necessary to change the return type of those methods from void to int and these changes must also be reflected in each overriding method in the derived classes.

The base class and each derived class are now contained within their own header file. These are added to the main program with #include directives but it is important to #include the base class before the derived classes to avoid a compiler error.

bird_capability.hpp

```cpp
#include <iostream>
using namespace std;

class Bird
{
  public:
    virtual int Talk() const { return -1; }   //error
    virtual int Fly()  const { return -1; }   //error
};
```

pigeon.hpp

```cpp
class Pigeon : public Bird
{
  public:
    virtual int Talk() const
    { cout << "COO! COO!\n"; return 0; }

    virtual int Fly()  const
    { cout << "Pigeon flies away...\n"; return 0;}

};
```

chicken.hpp

```cpp
class Chicken : public Bird
{
  public:
    virtual int Talk() const
      { cout << "CLUCK! CLUCK!\n"; return 0; }

    virtual int Fly()  const
    {
      cout << "I\'m just a chicken - I can\'t fly!\n";
      return 0;
    }
};
```

newbirds.cpp

```cpp
#include "bird_capability.hpp"  //order matters!
#include "pigeon.hpp"
#include "chicken.hpp"

int main()
{
  Bird *pPigeon = new Pigeon;    //declare pointers
  Bird *pChicken = new Chicken;
  pPigeon -> Talk();             //virtual method calls
  pPigeon -> Fly();
  pChicken -> Talk();
  pChicken -> Fly();
  pPigeon ->  Bird::Talk();      //explicit base calls
  pChicken -> Bird::Fly();
  pChicken -> Talk();            //virtual method call
  return 0;
}
```

Explicit calls to the base methods now generate no output but an error is signalled to the system that could be used to generate an error message – see Chapter 14 for more details on error-handling.

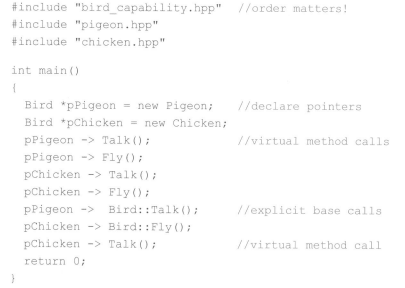

```
C:\MyPrograms>c++ newbirds.cpp -o newbirds.exe

C:\MyPrograms>newbirds
COO! COO!
Pigeon flies away...
CLUCK! CLUCK!
I'm just a chicken - I can't fly!
CLUCK! CLUCK!
```

Abstract data types

An abstract data type (ADT) represents a concept, rather than a tangible object, and is always the base to other classes. A base class can be made into an ADT by initializing one or more of its virtual methods with zero. These are then known as "pure virtual methods" and must always be overridden in derived classes.

The following example creates an ADT of its base Shape class. This has a derived class named Rect which overrides each pure virtual method. The Rect class in turn has a further derived class named Square.

adt.cpp

Remember that only one pure virtual method is needed in a class to designate it as an ADT.

```cpp
#include <iostream>
using namespace std;

class Shape
{
  public:   //use default constructor & destructor
    virtual int GetArea() = 0;   // pure virtual method
    virtual int GetPerim() = 0;  // pure virtual method
    virtual void Draw() = 0;      // pure virtual method
};

class Rect : public Shape
{
  public:            //constructor & destructor
    Rect(int initHeight, int initWidth)
      { Height = initHeight; Width = initWidth; }
    virtual ~Rect(){}
    virtual int GetArea() { return Height * Width; }
    virtual int GetPerim()
      {return (2 * Height) + (2 * Width); }
    virtual int GetHeight() { return Height; }
    virtual void Draw()
    {
      for (int i = 0; i < Height; i++)
      { for (int j = 0; j < Width; j++) cout << "x ";
        cout << "\n"; }
    }
  private:
    int Height, Width;
};
```

adt.cpp
(continued)

```cpp
class Square : public Rect
{
  public:    //create a single-argument constructor
     Square(int length) : Rect(length, length) { };
     ~Square(){}
     int GetPerim() { return 4 * GetHeight(); }
};

int main()
{
  Shape *pRect = new Rect(3, 7);  //declare pointers
  Shape *pSquare = new Square(5);
  pRect -> Draw();
  cout << "Area is " << pRect -> GetArea() << endl;
  cout << "Perimeter is " << pRect -> GetPerim()<<endl;
  pSquare -> Draw();
  cout << "Area is " << pSquare -> GetArea() << endl;
  cout << "Perimeter is " << pSquare -> GetPerim();
  cout << endl;
  return 0;
}
```

The derived Square class inherits all the properties of the Rect class plus it creates a single-argument constructor and it contains an overriding method for the GetPerim method. Note the syntax used to create the new constructor.

```
C:\ Command Prompt                           _ □ ✕

C:\MyPrograms>c++ adt.cpp -o adt.exe

C:\MyPrograms>adt

x x x x x x x
x x x x x x x
x x x x x x x
Area is 21
Perimeter is 20

x x x x x
x x x x x
x x x x x
x x x x x
x x x x x
Area is 25
Perimeter is 20
```

It is illegal to create an object of any class that is an ADT – trying to do so just causes a compiler error.

Complex hierarchies

It is sometimes desirable to derive ADTs from other ADTs to construct a complex hierarchy of classes. This provides greater flexibility and is perfectly acceptable providing each pure method is defined at some point in a derived class.

A complex hierarchy is demonstrated in the following example that begins by creating its base Country class as an ADT. This contains just one pure virtual method named Continent that is defined in each of two classes derived from the base class according to needs.

The EUmember class is only needed in the Europe class – the states of North America will never become members of the European Union.

The derived Europe class adds a pure virtual method named EUmember to create another ADT. It also adds another variable and an accessor method to retrieve its stored value.

A regular class named Uk is derived from the Europe class and its constructor assigns variable values. It also defines the EUmember method declared in the Europe class. Another regular class named Usa is derived from the Namerica class and its constructor simply assigns values to its variables.

The program listed on page 154 uses this hierarchy by creating pointers to the second-level classes of Europe and Namerica – at which point all methods have been declared and are available.

countries.hpp

```
#include <string>
#include <iostream>
using namespace std;

class Country        //ADT base class
{
  public:
    virtual void Continent() const = 0; //pure method
    //accessor methods
    virtual string GetName() { return name; }
    virtual string GetPop()  { return pop; }
    virtual string GetCurr() { return curr; }
  protected:
    string name;
    string pop;
    string curr;
};
```

countries.hpp
(continued)

```cpp
class Europe : public Country    //ADT derived class
{
  public:
    virtual bool EUmember() const = 0; //pure method
    virtual void Continent() const { cout<<"Europe\n";}
    virtual int GetEntry() const { return entry; };
  protected:
    int entry;
};

class Namerica : public Country //non-ADT derived class
{
  public:
    virtual void Continent() const
      { cout << "North America\n"; }    };

class Uk : public Europe
{
  public:
    Uk()              //constructor & destructor methods
    {
      name = "United Kingdom";
      pop = "58,789,194";
      curr = "Pound Sterling";
      entry = 1973;
    }
    ~Uk() { }
    virtual bool EUmember() const { return true; }
};

class Usa : public Namerica
{
  public:
    Usa()             //constructor & destructor methods
    {
      name = "United States of America";
      pop = "280,562,489";
      curr = "US Dollar";
    }
    ~Usa() { }
};
```

Countries such as Norway and Switzerland are, at the time of writing, not EU members – so their classes would define the EUmember method to return false.

Levels of abstraction

The example below #includes the header file listed in the previous example to illustrate the output generated by calling its methods via pointers to its second-level classes:

countries.cpp

```cpp
#include "countries.hpp"

int main()
{
  Europe *UK = new Uk;
  Namerica *USA = new Usa;

  cout << "Continent:\t";
  UK -> Continent();
  cout << "Country:\t" <<   UK -> GetName() << endl;
  cout << "Population:\t" << UK -> GetPop() << endl;
  cout << "Currency:\t" <<  UK -> GetCurr() << endl;
  if(UK -> EUmember())
  cout << "EU member since " << UK -> GetEntry();
  cout << endl << endl;

  cout << "Continent:\t";
  USA -> Continent();
  cout << "Country:\t" <<   USA -> GetName() << endl;
  cout << "Population:\t" << USA -> GetPop() << endl;
  cout << "Currency:\t" <<  USA -> GetCurr() << endl;
  cout << endl << endl;
  return 0;
}
```

The header classes for this program have two levels of abstraction – that of the base Country class and that of the derived Europe class. The number of levels of abstraction to create is determined simply by the program's requirements.

```
C:\ Command Prompt                          _ □ ✕

C:\MyPrograms>c++ countries.cpp -o countries.exe

C:\MyPrograms>countries
Continent:        Europe
Country:          United Kingdom
Population:       58,789,194
Currency:         Pound Sterling
EU member since 1973

Continent:        North America
Country:          United States of America
Population:       280,562,489
Currency:         US Dollar
```

Processing macros

This chapter explores how compiler directives can be added to C++ code in much the same way as the familiar #include directive. These are useful for string substitution, creating definitions, running macros and help in debugging. Examples demonstrate how to usefully add compiler directives to perform tasks before the compiler executes the C++ code itself.

Covers

Chapter Thirteen

The C++ preprocessor

Whenever the C++ compiler runs, it first calls upon its preprocessor to seek any compiler directives that may be included in the source code. Each of these begin with the # hash character and will be implemented to effectively modify the source code before it is actually compiled.

The changes made by compiler directives to the preprocessor create a new temporary file that is not normally seen. It is this temporary file that is used to compile the program, not the original source code file.

The temporary files created by the GNU C++ compiler can be saved for inspection by using the -save-temps command line switch. For instance, the command shown below asks the compiler to save the temporary files for a source code file named test.cpp:

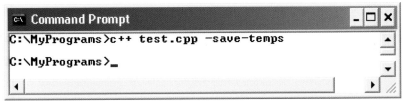

In this case two temporary files are created named test.ii and test.s whose contents can be viewed in any text editor. The test.s file contains low-level assembler instructions and the test.ii file recreates the original source code file but replaces an #include directive with detailed instructions that add the <iostream> class.

The contents of the generated temporary files are too large to reproduce here but you can use the simple hello.cpp file from page 12, with the -save-temps switch, to create your own temporary files for inspection in a text editor.

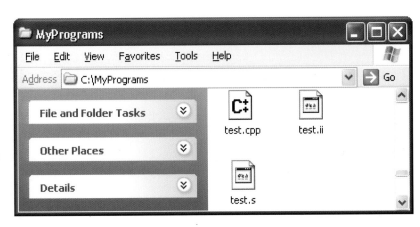

Defining substitutes

The #define compiler directive is used to specify an identifier and a string to be substituted by the preprocessor for each occurrence of the identifier in the source code. The following example defines an identifier named BOOK for a string containing the title of this book. Each occurrence of the BOOK identifier in the source code will be substituted for the string by the preprocessor.

defstring.cpp

```
#define BOOK "C++ Programming in easy steps"
#include <iostream>
using namespace std;

int main()
{
    cout << BOOK << endl;
    return 0;
}
```

The #define directive was seen earlier, on page 31 – remember that it is better to define constants with the const keyword because it provides type-checking that the preprocessor does not.

Running the preprocessor with the -save-temps switch, as described on the opposite page, creates a file named defstrings. ii whose contents can be viewed in a text editor. At the very end of this file, after the <iostream> inclusions, the #define and #include directives have disappeared and the string has indeed been substituted for the BOOK identifier.

```
Command Prompt                              _ □ X
C:\MyPrograms>c++ defstring.cpp -save-temps  ▲
C:\MyPrograms>_                              ▼
◀                                          ▶
```

```
defstring.ii - Notepad                    _ □ X
File  Edit  Format  View  Help
using namespace std;                      ▲

int main()
{
    cout << "C++ Programming in easy steps" << endl;
    return 0;
}                                         ▼
```

Conditional definitions

The #ifdef directive allows a conditional test to be made to see if a particular string has already been defined. Action to be taken if the test evaluates to true can then be declared as a statement block. The block is terminated by a final #endif directive.

Similarly an #ifndef directive tests whether a string has <u>not</u> been previously defined. When this evaluates to true its statement block will be executed. This must also end with a final #endif directive.

The #ifndef directive is the logical reverse of the #ifdef directive.

The following example tests to see if strings with BOOK and AUTHOR identifiers have been defined and outputs appropriate messages according to the test results:

ifdef.cpp

```
#define BOOK "C++ Programming in easy steps"
#include <iostream>
using namespace std;

int main()
{
  #ifdef BOOK
    cout << "BOOK defined\n";
  #endif

  #ifndef AUTHOR
   cout << "AUTHOR not defined\n";
  #endif

  return 0;
}
```

A definition can be removed at any time with an #undef directive.

```
Command Prompt                                    _ □ ✕
C:\MyPrograms>c++ ifdef.cpp -o ifdef.exe

C:\MyPrograms>ifdef
BOOK defined
AUTHOR not defined
```

Providing alternatives

As might be expected there is also an #else directive that can be used to specify alternative code to be executed in an #ifdef block or in an #ifndef block. Each block must end, as usual, with a final #endif directive.

The example below uses #else directives in an #ifdef block relating to the definition of a platform version of Windows. Notice that it is enough to simply #define an identifier without any string to create a valid definition.

else.cpp

Notice that #ifdef blocks can be nested – as seen in this example.

```
#define WINDOWS
#define XP
#include <iostream>
using namespace std;

int main()
{
  cout << "Platform is ";
  #ifdef WINDOWS
      #ifdef NT
        cout << "Windows NT\n";
      #endif

      #ifdef XP
        cout << "Windows XP\n";
      #else
        cout << "Windows 9x\n";
    #endif
  #endif
  return 0;
}
```

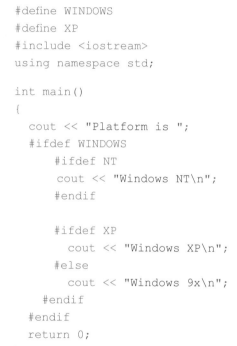

```
C:\MyPrograms>c++ else.cpp -o else.exe

C:\MyPrograms>else
Platform is Windows XP
```

Inclusion guards

C++ programs typically comprise many .hpp header files and a .cpp implementation file containing the main program. Many of the header files may contain classes derived from a base class so must be able to access the base class file in order to compile. It is easy, therefore, to #include the same base class file in more than one derived class header file – but this is not allowed.

The popular solution to this problem uses compiler directives to check if the base class header file has already been included. If not then an #include directive can safely add it.

An earlier example from pages 148–149 can be modified to demonstrate how these "inclusion guards" work. The current code clumsily makes the base class available to the derived classes by prior inclusion in the implementation file. Imagine a much larger program with lots more header files!

Leaving the bird_capability.hpp base class unchanged, the derived class pigeon.hpp can be modified by adding compiler directives.

pigeon2.hpp

```
#ifndef BIRD_CAPABILITY_HPP
#define  BIRD_CAPABILITY_HPP
#include "bird_capability.hpp"
#endif

class Pigeon : public Bird
{
  public:
    virtual int Talk() const
      { cout << "COO! COO!\n"; return 0; }
    virtual int Fly()  const
      { cout << "Pigeon flies away...\n"; return 0;}
};
```

Although the identifier for another header file could technically have any name, traditionally it is an uppercase version of the file name with the dot changed to an underscore character. If the base class header file has not already been included the #ifndef test will return false. This means that the #define directive will then define that identifier and the #include directive will include the base class header file.

The original header file chicken.hpp is listed earlier on page 149.

The same compiler directives can also be inserted into the chicken.hpp derived class header file to test if the base class header file is already included. Both derived class files are saved with a "2" appended to their file name to avoid overwriting the originals.

Now the implementation file need not #include the bird_capability.hpp header file because it is already included in one of the derived class files.

newbirds2.cpp

```cpp
#include "pigeon2.hpp"
#include "chicken2.hpp"

int main()
{
  Bird *pPigeon = new Pigeon;    //declare pointers
  Bird *pChicken = new Chicken;
  pPigeon -> Talk();             //virtual method calls
  pPigeon -> Fly();
  pChicken -> Talk();
  pChicken -> Fly();
  pPigeon ->  Bird::Talk();      //explicit base calls
  pChicken -> Bird::Fly();
  pChicken -> Talk();
  return 0;
}
```

The pigeon2.hpp file is included first so that will define and include the base class. When the chicken2.hpp file is included it finds that the base class is already defined so does not define it again.

The modified program executes exactly as before but this is a far better technique that should be employed throughout all programs. Its benefits will be much appreciated, especially in larger programs, and can often save hours of debugging time.

```
C:\MyPrograms>c++ newbirds2.cpp -o newbirds2.exe

C:\MyPrograms>newbirds2
COO! COO!
Pigeon flies away...
CLUCK! CLUCK!
I'm just a chicken - I can't fly!
CLUCK! CLUCK!
```

Macro functions

The #define directive can be used to create macro functions which will be substituted in the source code before it is compiled.

The function declaration comprises the identifier name immediately followed by a pair of parentheses containing the function's arguments – it is important not to leave any space between the identifier name and the parentheses. This is then followed by a space, then the function definition within another pair of parentheses.

The convention is to use uppercase for macro names.

For instance, the syntax to declare and define a function to half an argument value could look like this:

```
#define HALF(n) (n / 2)
```

The example below declares and defines four macro functions which are each substituted once in the main program code. The output is illustrated at the top of the opposite page.

macro.cpp

```cpp
#define CUBE(n) (n * n * n)
#define SQUARE(n) (n * n)
#define MIN(n1, n2) (n1 < n2 ? n1 : n2)
#define MAX(n1, n2) (n1 > n2 ? n1 : n2)

#include <iostream>
using namespace std;

int main()
{
  int x = 8, y = 16;

  cout << x << " cubed:\t";
  cout << CUBE(x) << endl;
  cout << x << " squared:\t";
  cout << SQUARE(x) << endl;
  cout << x << "," << y << "  max:\t";
  cout << MAX(x, y) << endl;
  cout << x << "," << y << "  min:\t";
  cout << MIN(x, y) << endl;
  return 0;
}
```

```
Command Prompt                              _ □ ×
C:\MyPrograms>c++ macro.cpp -o macro.exe

C:\MyPrograms>macro
8 cubed:        512
8 squared:      64
8,16  max:      16
8,16  min:      8
```

Care should be taken when using macro functions because, unlike regular C++ functions, they do not perform any kind of type checking – so it is easy to create a macro that causes errors. On the other hand, because macros substitute the function inline they avoid the overhead of a function call – so the program runs faster.

The substitution of the macro functions in the example above can be seen at the end of the intermediate file, as shown below:

```
Command Prompt                              _ □ ×
C:\MyPrograms>c++ macro.cpp -save-temps

C:\MyPrograms>_
```

```
macro.ii - Notepad                          _ □ ×
File  Edit  Format  View  Help
int main()
{
  int x = 8, y = 16;

  cout << x << " cubed:\t";
  cout << (x * x * x) << endl;
  cout << x << " squared:\t";
  cout << (x * x) << endl;
  cout << x << "," << y << "  max:\t";
  cout << (x > y ? x : y) << endl;
  cout << x << "," << y << "  min:\t";
  cout << (x < y ? x : y) << endl;
  return 0;
}
```

String manipulation

The preprocessor # operator is known as the "stringizing" operator as it substitutes a string, within double quotes, of whatever follows its declaration up to the next whitespace.

This operator is useful to pass string arguments to a preprocessor #define function without needing to surround each string with double quotes.

In the example below each string that is passed as the argument to the preprocessor #define function named LINEOUT is surrounded with double quotes by the stringizing operator. This allows the cout function to output each string successfully along with a final newline character.

Notice how the code appears more compact because the LINEOUT function neatly avoids the need to type the repeated cout function calls in full.

lineout.cpp

```
#define LINEOUT(str) cout << #str << endl

#include <iostream>
using namespace std;

int main()
{
LINEOUT(\nIn a bowl to sea went wise men three);
LINEOUT(On a brilliant night in June:);
LINEOUT(They carried a net and their hearts were set);
LINEOUT(On fishing up the moon.);
return 0;
}
```

```
Command Prompt                                    _ □ ✕
C:\MyPrograms>c++ lineout.cpp -o lineout.exe

C:\MyPrograms>lineout

In a bowl to sea went wise men three
On a brilliant night in June:
They carried a net and their hearts were set
On fishing up the moon.
```

The preprocessor ## concatenation operator joins together two terms into a single word. It is used in the example below to join the Type argument value to the word "Ball". Each concatenated word is then used to create a new class of the Ball type, and to call the relevant class's getDiameter accessor method.

concatdef.cpp

```cpp
#define NewBall(Type, Size) Ball Type ## Ball(Size)
#define BallSize(Type) Type ## Ball.getDiameter()
#include <iostream>
using namespace std;

class Ball
{
  public:
    Ball(float size) { diameter = size; }
    ~Ball() { }
    float getDiameter() const { return diameter; }
  protected:
    float diameter;
};

int main()
{
  NewBall(Snooker, 52.4);
  NewBall(Tennis, 65.7);
  cout << "Snooker ball diameter is ";
  cout << BallSize(Snooker) << endl;
  cout << "Tennis ball diameter is ";
  cout << BallSize(Tennis) << endl;
  return 0;
}
```

```
Command Prompt                                    _ □ ×
C:\MyPrograms>c++ concatdef.cpp -o concatdef.exe

C:\MyPrograms>concatdef
Snooker ball diameter is 52.4mm
Tennis ball diameter is 65.7mm
```

Assert debugging

It can sometimes be helpful to use compiler directives to assist with debugging program code. The GNU C++ compiler includes a built-in function named assert that can be used to test the expected value of variables, pointers and strings. This function return true when its argument evaluates to true or it returns false otherwise.

Other compilers may not have an intrinsic assert function and may therefore require a custom one.

For instance, this statement checks that a variable named x contains a value of less than 5:

```
assert(x < 5);
```

Alternatively a custom ASSERT function can be #defined for this purpose. In either case the preprocessor should ignore all assert statements when DEBUG is not defined. This means that program code can be liberally sprinkled with assert statements to check its performance – then debugging can be turned off simply by commenting out the DEBUG definition.

The example on the opposite page demonstrates how a custom ASSERT function can be used to test the value of a variable.

The definition of the ASSERT function can be spread over several lines if each line is terminated with a backslash escape character. This technique can be used with any compiler directive.

Each call to this ASSERT function passes an argument value of true or false that determines the generated message. When the evaluated expression returns true the message simply states that the test was passed. When the evaluated expression returns false the function provides details about the failure.

This example makes good use of some predefined preprocessor macros named __DATE__, __TIME__, __FILE__ and __LINE__ to describe how the ASSERT test has failed. Notice that these macros are prefixed by <u>two</u> underscore characters and also suffixed by <u>two</u> underscore characters. This ensures that they are unlikely to conflict with other names used in the program.

Predictably __DATE__ returns the current date, __TIME__ returns the current time, __FILE__ returns the file name and __LINE__ returns the line number where the failure occurred.

assert.cpp

```cpp
#define DEBUG
#include <iostream>
using namespace std;

#ifndef DEBUG
#define ASSERT(n)
#else
#define ASSERT(n) \
if(!n) \
{ \
  cout << #n << " - Failed\n"; \
  cout << "on " << __DATE__ ; \
  cout << " at " << __TIME__ << endl; \
  cout << "in file " << __FILE__ ; \
  cout << " at line " << __LINE__ << endl; \
} \
else cout << #n << " - Passed\n";
#endif


int main()
{
  bool flag = 1;
  cout << "\nFirst assert: ";
  ASSERT(flag == true);
  cout << "\nSecond assert: ";
  ASSERT(flag != true);
  return 0;
}
```

```
C:\ Command Prompt                                    _ □ ✕

C:\MyPrograms>c++ assert.cpp -o assert.exe

C:\MyPrograms>assert

First assert: flag == true - Passed

Second assert: flag != true - Failed
on Feb  3 2005 at 14:40:08
in file assert.cpp at line 29
```

Debugging levels

A greater degree of debugging control can be achieved by specifying different levels that each #define how a custom ASSERT function should operate. The example below uses the #elif compiler directive in a preprocessor statement block that #defines three different levels. In this case the highest DEBUG level is used but this can be changed by altering its defined value.

debug.cpp

```
#include <iostream>
using namespace std;
#define DEBUG 2       // 0 = OFF, 1 = LOW, 2 = HIGH
#if DEBUG == 0
  #define ASSERT(n)
#elif DEBUG == 1
  #define ASSERT(n) \
  if(!n) { cout << #n << " - Failed\n"; }
#elif DEBUG == 2
  #define ASSERT(n) \
  if(!n) { cout << #n << " - Failed at line "; \
          cout << __LINE__ << endl; } \
          else cout << #n << " - Passed\n";
#endif

int main()
{
  bool flag = 1;
  cout << "\nFirst assert: ";
  ASSERT(flag == true);
  cout << "\nSecond assert: ";
  ASSERT(flag != true);
  return 0;
}
```

The #elif preprocessor directive is the equivalent to else if in C++.

```
Command Prompt                              _ □ ×
C:\MyPrograms>c++ debug.cpp -o debug.exe

C:\MyPrograms>debug

First assert: flag == true - Passed

Second assert: flag != true - Failed at line 27
```

Handling exceptions

This chapter demonstrates how to recognize an exceptional error that occurs at run-time. It lists some C++ standard exceptions and illustrates how they can be used to make a program more robust. The importance of consistent coding style to prevent errors is also discussed.

Covers

Chapter Fourteen

Errors and exceptions

Despite the best efforts of the programmer, C++ programs may, unfortunately, contain one or more of these three type of bugs:

- Logic errors – the code is syntactically correct but attempts to perform an operation that is illogical. For instance, the program may attempt to divide a number by zero, causing an error.

- Syntax errors – the code contains incorrect use of the C++ language. For instance, an opening brace does not have a matching closing brace.

- Exceptional errors – the program runs as expected until an exceptional condition is encountered that crashes the program. For instance, a program may ask the user to enter a number which the user enters in word form rather than in numeric form.

The C++ standards allow the compiler to spot "compile-time" errors involving logic and syntax but the possibility of exceptional errors is more difficult to locate as they only occur at "run-time". This means that the programmer must try to predict problems that may arise and prepare to handle those exceptional errors.

The first step is to identify which part of the program code may, under certain conditions, cause an exceptional error. This can then be surrounded by a try block that uses the try keyword then encloses the suspect code within a pair of braces.

When an exceptional error occurs the try block then "throws" the exception out to a catch block which immediately follows the try block. This uses the catch keyword then encloses statements describing how to handle the exception within a pair of braces.

In the example on the opposite page, the try block calls a function and passes an integer argument to be used to create an exception.

The throw function manually throws an exception to the catch block exception handler when the loop reaches the argument value.

In this case it also passes the value causing the exception as an argument back to the catch block so it can report the troublesome value in its generated output message.

try.cpp

```cpp
#include <iostream>
using namespace std;

void printSequence(int stopNum);  //handler prototype

int main()
{
  try
  {
    printSequence(10);    //call function
  }
  catch(int thrownNum)    //catch thrown exceptions
  {
    cout << "Caught an exception with value: ";
    cout << thrownNum << endl;
  }
  return 0;
}

void printSequence(int stopNum)
{
  for(int num = 1; num < 21; num++)
  {
    if (num >= stopNum) throw(num);  //throw exception
    else cout << "Number: " << num << endl;
  }
}
```

When an exception is thrown control passes to the catch block.

```
Command Prompt                                    _ □ ✕

C:\MyPrograms>c++ try.cpp -o try.exe

C:\MyPrograms>try
Number: 1
Number: 2
Number: 3
Number: 4
Number: 5
Number: 6
Number: 7
Number: 8
Number: 9
Caught an exception with value: 10
```

Exception objects

C++ compilers have intrinsic exception objects that describe the kind of exception that has occurred. The appropriate object is automatically thrown when an exception occurs within a try block. A reference to the exception object can be passed to the catch block – conventionally this is named "e". To retrieve exception messages the exception object has a method named what – so e.what() returns the actual message.

The precise message varies on each compiler and some are more clear than others. A comparison of messages can be seen in the following example that displays output from the same program run with the GNU C++ compiler and in Microsoft Visual C++ 6.0. This exception is caused by the program attempting to erase characters 4 to 6 from a string that only has 3 characters.

excep.cpp

```
#include <iostream>
using namespace std;

int main ()
{
  string str = "C++";
  try
  { str.erase(4, 6); }
  catch(exception &e)
  { cout << "Exception: " << e.what() << endl; }
  return 0;
}
```

```
Command Prompt                                    _ □ ✕
C:\MyPrograms>c++ excep.cpp -o excep.exe

C:\MyPrograms>excep
Exception: basic_string::_M_check
```

```
Command Prompt                                    _ □ ✕
C:\MyPrograms\Debug>excep
Exception: invalid string position
```

Standard exceptions

The C++ <stdexcept> header file defines a number of exception classes. Its base class is named exception from which are derived other classes that categorize a number of common exceptions.

Each of the main classes are listed in the table below which illustrates their relationship. Notice that further classes are derived from both the logic_error and runtime_error derived classes.

Class	Purpose
exception	base class
logic_error	derived class for logic errors
domain_error	violation of precondition
invalid_argument	invalid argument in throwing function
length_error	object too long
out_of_range	invalid range request
runtime_error	derived class for runtime errors
range_error	violation of a postcondition
overflow_error	arithmetic overflow
bad_alloc	failure allocating storage
bad_cast	invalid dynamic cast
bad_typeid	null pointer in an expression

The example on the next page illustrates the use of standard exceptions.

When the <stdexcept> header is #included in a program the standard exception classes can be used to identify the type of exception thrown to a catch block.

Simply add the exact exception class name in the parentheses following the catch keyword.

Multiple catch blocks can be used in succession, much like case statements in a switch block, to test for several different types of exception. The equivalent of the switch block's default keyword in this case is the "ellipsis" – that is, just three dots within the parentheses following the catch keyword, such as catch(...). This should be used in the final catch block to execute its code when the previously sought exceptions are not found.

Using standard exceptions

The example below demonstrates how the standard exceptions, described on the previous page, can be used to identify the kind of exception that has occurred.

Notice that the out_of_range exception in this case is caught by its base class logic_error. Deleting, or commenting-out, that first catch block would allow the exception to be caught as an out_of_range exception by the next catch block.

stdexcept.cpp

```
#include <stdexcept>          //access standard exceptions
#include <iostream>
using namespace std;

int main ()
{
  string str;

  try
  {
    str.replace(100,1,1,'c');
  }
  catch(logic_error)
  { cout << "Exception: Logic error\n"; }
  catch (out_of_range)
  { cout << "Exception: Out of range\n"; }
  catch (overflow_error)
  { cout << "Exception: Overflow error\n"; }
  catch(...)
  { cout << "Exception: Unidentified error\n"; }
  return 0;

}
```

Notice that the compiler generates a warning to let you know that the out_of_range exception will be caught by its base class logic_error.

```
Command Prompt                                    _ □ ✕
C:\MyPrograms>c++ stdexcept.cpp -o stdexcept.exe
stdexcept.cpp: In function `int main()':
stdexcept.cpp:20: warning: exception of type `std::
stdexcept.cpp:16: warning:     by earlier handler fo

C:\MyPrograms>stdexcept
Exception: Logic error
```

When an exception occurs the exception handler should at least prevent the program from crashing. It may also advise the user about the error then exit gracefully, or inform the user and recover, or correct the error and continue without disturbing the user. The best method is dictated by circumstances. The example below elects to advise the user about an error then continue. This can be changed to stop the program immediately after advising the error by simply uncommenting the indicated line.

recover.cpp

```cpp
#include <stdexcept>
#include <string>
#include <iostream>
using namespace std;

int main ()
{
  string str = "C++";
  cout << "String is " << str << endl;
  try
  { str.erase(4, 6); }
  catch(out_of_range)
  {
    cout << "Exception: Out of range - handled. ";
    //uncomment the next line to stop the program
    //return -1;
    cout << "Continuing...\n";
  }
  str += " Programming in easy steps\n";
  cout << "String is " << str << endl;
  return 0;
}
```

Add a final catch block with an ellipsis argument to catch all other forms of exceptions.

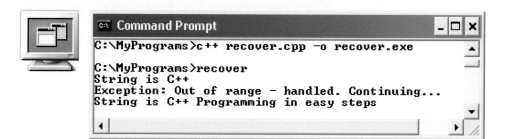

```
C:\MyPrograms>c++ recover.cpp -o recover.exe

C:\MyPrograms>recover
String is C++
Exception: Out of range - handled. Continuing...
String is C++ Programming in easy steps
```

Styling to prevent errors

The best way to avoid creating bugs in your C++ programs is to write clear consistently-styled code. Code styling is a very personal taste but mainly involves the use of whitespace to make the code more easily readable.

One of the biggest style decisions concerns the way that braces should be formatted. Many C++ programmers insist that each opening brace should appear at the end of other code on one line, but each closing brace should appear on its own line, like this:

```
if(5 > 1){
   if('A' == 'A')
      if(1 != 0){
         doSomething();
      }
   }
}
```

It is also acceptable to enclose short statements within braces on a single line.

This book recommends the style used in the example code listings so that each brace appears on its own line aligned in matching columns, like this:

```
if(5 > 1)
{
   if('A' == 'A')

      if(1 != 0)
      {
         doSomething();
      }
   }
}
```

Did you spot the missing brace in the first style of coding?

Both these examples are missing an opening brace after the second conditional if test – but it's more obvious with the second style of coding. The extra whitespace costs nothing but makes the code clearer. Whatever personal style you adopt for naming conventions, braces, indentation, and so on, it is important to use that style consistently. This helps prevent errors and saves you time by making it easier to find those bugs that do slip through.

Moving on

After developing an understanding of the basics of C++
the next inevitable step is to move on to graphical C++
programming with an Integrated Development Environment
(IDE) like Microsoft Visual C++. This chapter develops a
random number generator as a traditional console application
then illustrates how the same program can be used to create a
graphical program in a Windows environment.

Covers

Chapter Fifteen

A random number generator

The rand function generates a "random" positive integer from 0 to a large value (at least 32,767) every time it is called. To set a range for the random numbers use the modulus operator to specify a maximum value. For instance, to set a range from 0 to 9:

```
int r = (rand() % 9) + 1;
```

The numbers generated by rand are not truly random as the function generates the same sequence of numbers each time the program is executed. In order for rand to generate a different sequence of numbers the "seed" that starts the sequence must be specified. This is achieved by specifying an integer argument to a function named srand, like this:

The srand function must only be used once in a program.

```
srand(12345);
```

Setting the random seed with srand at the beginning of a program ensures that calls to the rand function will no longer generate the default sequence of numbers. However, although it will generate a different sequence, it is still one that will be repeated each time the program is executed.

To generate a more random sequence the argument to the srand function must be something other than a static integer. It is commonplace to seed the rand function using the current time as the argument to srand, like this:

The time function is part of the <ctime> standard header file. It returns the current system time expressed in seconds after the epoch at 00:00:00 GMT on January 1, 1970. This means that the same sequence of numbers can be generated if the program is executed more than once within the same second.

```
srand(time(NULL));
```

Now the sequence of numbers generated by rand will be different on each occasion that the program is executed.

The example program on the opposite page uses the current time to seed the random number generator. It creates an array of integers, in order, from 0 to 49. Random numbers generated by rand, in a range of 1 to 49, are shuffled in array elements 1 to 49. This means that the array elements 1 to 49 contain all the numbers 1 to 49, in a random order, without repeating any number – element 0 always contains a zero value.

The program selects the values in elements 1 to 6 to represent a random selection of six numbers that could be an entry in the weekly UK lottery prize draw.

lotto.cpp

The itoa function converts an int to a string and takes three arguments to specify the number to convert, the string variable to which the converted number should be assigned and the base to use for the conversion. For instance, a base of 10 converts to decimal.

This useful function is widely used but is not part of ANSI C++ so may not be supported by all compilers.

```cpp
#include <ctime>    //include for time function
#include <iostream>
using namespace std;

int main()
{
  char buffer[3];   //character buffer
  int i, r, temp;   //integer variables
  int nums[50];     //50 number array, elements 0-49

  //random seed of current time in 1-second precision
  srand(time(NULL));

  //fill number elements 1-49 with values 1-49
  for(i = 1; i < 50; i++)   nums[i] = i;

  //algorithm to randomize values in elements 1-49
  for(i = 1; i < 50; i++)
  {
    r = (rand() % 49) + 1;
    temp = nums[i]; nums[i] = nums[r]; nums[r] = temp;
  }

  //write 6 array number values
  cout << "Your six Lucky Numbers are...\n";
  cout << itoa(nums[1], buffer, 10) << "    ";
  cout << itoa(nums[2], buffer, 10) << "    ";
  cout << itoa(nums[3], buffer, 10) << "    ";
  cout << itoa(nums[4], buffer, 10) << "    ";
  cout << itoa(nums[5], buffer, 10) << "    ";
  cout << itoa(nums[6], buffer, 10) << "    ";
  cout << endl;
  return 0;
}
```

```
Command Prompt
C:\MyPrograms>c++ lotto.cpp -o lotto.exe

C:\MyPrograms>lotto
Your six Lucky Numbers are...
2    18    44    27    17    49
```

C++ programming in Windows

C++ Builder is another popular IDE – it's easier to use than Visual C++ but requires a large support file to be included with program distribution. You can discover more about C++ Builder at www.borland.com.

The most widely used professional environment for C++ development is the Microsoft Visual C++ IDE. It is more difficult to use than some other IDEs but offers a great advantage when developing software for Windows – the runtime support files needed by C++ executable programs are shipped as part of the Windows platform. This means that distribution of programs developed with Visual C++ need not include hefty support files because they are already on the user's system.

A comprehensive exploration of Visual C++ is beyond the remit of this book but it is appropriate to demonstrate how the random number generator program listed on the previous page can be made into a graphical Windows program quite easily.

When starting a new project in Visual C++ you must first select the type of project and give it a name in the New dialog. The MFC AppWizard, chosen below, is a great start for most programs.

The AppWizard automatically generates all the code to create a complete basic windowed application. This can be immediately compiled and run to produce a Window with default controls.

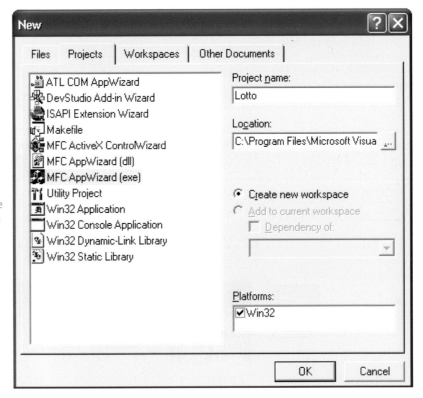

Selecting the option to create a Dialog Based application in the next dialog generates a number of standard project files and a graphic "form" to be used as the program interface. By default this form contains two button controls and a static text control box:

The dotted grid is only there to act as an aid in positioning controls
– it does not appear in the final application window.

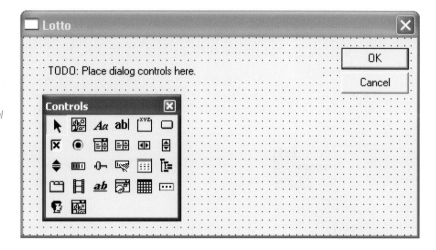

The default controls can be deleted, then new controls added to the form by dragging them from the Controls palette. For instance, the default form below has been re-sized and three "picture" controls have been added to display bitmaps.

Turn to the next page to discover how to add the code to complete this windowed application.

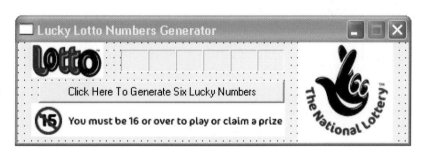

A "button" control has also been added together with six "static text" controls. The button will be used to execute the random number generator and the generated six numbers will be displayed in the static text boxes.

Adding functional code

The application form created on the previous page can be compiled and run by clicking buttons on the Visual C++ tool bar. This will produce a dialog-style Window with the controls that have been added but clicking the button control will have no effect until code is added to make the program functional.

Back in the design view of the form the button control has been named "ClickMe". A double-click on the button control opens the source code editor at an empty function named OnClickMe. This is where the random number generator code can be added to specify what should happen when the button is clicked.

(fragment from) LottoDlg.cpp

```
void CLottoDlg::OnClickMe()
{
    char buffer[2];         //character buffer
    int i, r, temp;         //integer variables
    int nums[50];           //array for 50 (elements 0-49)

    //random seed based on time to millisecond precision
    SYSTEMTIME  *pSt = new SYSTEMTIME;
    GetSystemTime(pSt);
    srand(pSt -> wMilliseconds);

    //fill number elements 1-49 with values 1-49
    for(i = 1; i < 50; i++)   nums[i]=i;

    //algorithm to randomize values in elements 1-49
    for(i = 1; i < 50; i++)
    {
        r = (rand() % 49) + 1;
        temp = nums[i]; nums[i] = nums[r]; nums[r] = temp;
    }

    //write 6 array number values on labels
    m_label1 = itoa(nums[1], buffer, 10);
    m_label2 = itoa(nums[2], buffer, 10);
    m_label3 = itoa(nums[3], buffer, 10);
    m_label4 = itoa(nums[4], buffer, 10);
    m_label5 = itoa(nums[5], buffer, 10);
    m_label6 = itoa(nums[6], buffer, 10);
    UpdateData(FALSE);
}
```

Although the SYSTEMTIME object will be unfamiliar you should be able to recognize how it is being used: a pointer to a new SYSTEMTIME object is created, then assigned the current system time. Its wMilliseconds member can then be accessed to retrieve the millisecond component of the stored time.

The code inserted into the OnClickMe function is the same as that used for the console application on page 179 with three changes.

Firstly, because this is a Windows application, the program can communicate directly with the Windows Application Programming Interface (WinAPI) to seed the rand function to millisecond precision. This allows the program to be executed many times per second without the random sequence repeating.

The WinAPI can be used to communicate with Windows by any programming language that can access the API, including Java, C, Visual Basic and, of course, the C++ language.

Secondly, the static text controls, named m_label1 - m_label6, are assigned the value of the six elements in the randomized array, instead of having cout display them as standard output.

Finally, the UpdateData function call refreshes the application window to reveal the newly assigned values. This replaces the final return statement in the console application.

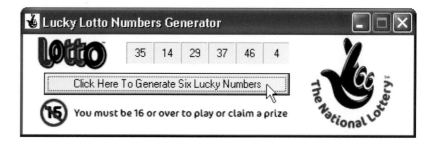

To paint in a Windows application you must first get a "device context".

Notice that the background color in the application window above is white, to match the background of the bitmap pictures. To achieve this requires a fragment of code to be added to the default OnPaint function. It contains a single if - else statement in which the else block is empty. This is where the following code can be added to "paint" the form's background:

(fragment from) LottoDlg.cpp

```
CPaintDC dc(this);
CRect rect;
GetClientRect(rect);
dc.FillSolidRect(rect, RGB(255,255,255));
```

This example will, hopefully, have given you a taste for Windows programming and illustrate how easy it can be to create programs.

The standard C++ library

The tables on these two pages list each of the header files included with the GNU C++ compiler, together with a brief description of their purpose.

The 13 headers marked with a * make up the C++ Standard Template Library (STL).

\<algorithm\> *	defines some useful algorithms
\<bitset\>	administers sets of bits
\<complex\>	performs complex arithmetic
\<deque\> *	implements a deque container
\<exception\>	controls exception handling
\<fstream\>	manipulates external streams
\<functional\> *	constructs function objects
\<iomanip\>	iostream manipulators that take an argument
\<ios\>	a template base class for iostream classes
\<iosfwd\>	allows undefined iostream template classes
\<iostream\>	iostream objects to manipulate standard streams
\<istream\>	performs extractions
\<iterator\> *	templates that helps define and manipulate iterators
\<limits\>	tests numeric type properties
\<list\> *	implements a list container
\<locale\>	controls locale-specific behavior
\<map\> *	implements associative containers
\<memory\> *	allocates and frees storage for various containers
\<new\>	functions that allocate and free storage
\<numeric\> *	provides useful numeric functions
\<ostream\>	performs insertions
\<queue\> *	implements a queue container
\<set\> *	implements containers with unique elements
\<sstream\>	manipulates string containers
\<stack\> *	implements a stack container

<stdexcept>	reports exceptions
<streambuf>	provides a buffer for iostream operations
<string>	implements a string container
<typeinfo>	reports the result of the typeid operator
<utility> *	provides general utility operations
<valarray>	supports value-oriented arrays
<vector> *	implements a vector container
<cassert>	enforces assertions when functions execute
<cctype>	classifies characters
<cerrno>	tests error codes reported by library functions
<cfloat>	tests floating-point type properties
<ciso646>	supports ISO 646 variant character sets
<climits>	tests integer type properties
<clocale>	supports different cultural conventions
<cmath>	provides common mathematical functions
<csetjump>	executes non-local goto statements
<csignal>	controls various exceptional conditions
<cstdarg>	accesses a varying number of arguments
<cstddef>	defines several useful types and macros
<cstdio>	provides input and output operations
<cstdlib>	provides a variety of basic operations
<cstring>	manipulates several kinds of strings
<ctime>	provides various time and date formats
<cwchar>	manipulates wide streams
<cwctype>	classifies wide characters

The final 18 headers in this table are taken from the C language and prefix their former name with a "c" to denote their origin. Some of these have been slightly modified for use in C++.

The "Help" section of C++ IDEs includes a comprehensive reference of all C++ headers and each of their methods.

Useful C++ resources

This book will, hopefully, have given you a good understanding of the basics of C++ to the ANSI C++ standard. Like any language, be it a spoken language or a programming language, the best way to become proficient is to practice using it.

www.devx.com

There are many helpful C++ resources available on the Internet. Probably the best independent developer website is DevX which provides tutorials, articles, product reviews and source code. They also have a useful archive of tips submitted by C++ developers and have a special section named "Get Help with C/C++" where you can search a database of answers to programming topics. DevX offer a free development newsletter delivering tips, information, services, how-to articles, expert advice, special offers and more.

www.cplusplus.com

Another great C++ resource is the Cplusplus Resources website. In addition to general C++ information and source code this site has some forums where you can seek help about C++ issues. The forums are separated into categories for "General", "Beginners", "ANSI C++/STL", "Windows", "Mac" and "Unix/Linux".

More C++ forums can be found at www.tek-tips.com which awards points to resident experts who compete to be the top expert. This helps ensure the speed and quality of response to questions posed on these forums. There are specialist forums for "C++:Microsoft" and "Microsoft:Visual C++". Usefully the Tek-Tips forums are monitored to prevent promotional postings.

If you prefer to see information on a printed page you could subscribe to the monthly C/C++ Users Journal magazine which provides technical information to advanced professional developers. This focuses on practical solutions to complex C/C++ programming problems. It's produced in California but they accept subscribers from around the world. Their website, www.cuj.com, is well worth visiting as it contains some archived past articles and source code. There is also the "C++ Experts Forum" which is a monthly supplement to the magazine featuring columns by experts in C++.

There are many more useful C++ resources available on the Web which can be located using any search engine. This is testament to the huge popularity that C++ enjoys and these resources can help improve your own C++ skills. Happy C++ programming!

Index

fill   83
fixed   83
hex   82
internal   82
left   82
noboolalpha   82
noshowbase   82
noshowpoint   82
noshowpos   82
noskipws   82
nouppercase   83
oct   82
right   82
scientific   83
setfill   83
setprecision   83
setw   83
showbase   82
showpoint   82
showpos   82
skipws   82
uppercase   83
width   83
Int data type   19

L

L-value   115
Labels   56
Length of a string   62
Less than operator, <   40
Logic errors   170–171
Logical operators
   AND operator, &&   36
   NOT operator, !   36
   OR operator, || 36
Loops
   do-while   53
   for   50–51
   while   52

M

Macro functions   162–163
Main program
   main function   12
Members of a class   98
Memory   22
   address   114, 116
MFC AppWizard   180
Microsoft Visual C++   180
Millisecond precision   182
Minimalist GNU for Windows (MinGW)   11
Modulus operator, %   34
Multiplication operator, *   34

N

Nesting if statements   47
Newline
   \n escape sequence   20
   endl keyword   20
NOT operator, !   36
Null value   132

O

Object methods   101
Object-Oriented Programming (OOP)   144
Objects   100
OnClickMe function   183
OnPaint function   183
Operators
   arithmetical   34–35
   assignment   38–39
   comparison   40–41